Rollover Trucker

An Introduction to the Transportation Industry

By R. Dawn Weir

I0487357

I would like to thank Steve Badgley for his unwavering assistance and support. If not for Steve, I would most likely still be trying to figure out how to publish!

Look for Steve's work and other publications at:

WWW.BadgleyPublishingCompany.com

I would also like to thank my family and friends who believed in me. I am especially grateful to my loving husband, Clayton who has given me unwavering support and has encouraged me to keep writing.

To all of my readers who have encouraged me to keep writing and asking for more, I would like to thank you for encouraging me to write more. I will work hard to keep you entertained!

Introduction

This memoir is for anyone who has ever wondered what it was like to be a trucker, anyone who is considering a career in the trucking industry, and for my fellow drivers out there who are still trucking.

This book is meant to be entertaining and informative. It provides useful information, from the viewpoint of team drivers who were blessed to be given the opportunity to drive an eighteen wheeler. The information given is solely based on our personal experiences. As all truckers can attest, one driver's experiences on the road may not apply to all drivers. The purpose of this memoir is to share our experiences on the road, and help future drivers. It is especially written to give our fellow drivers a few laughs and boosts of encouragement. In addition, this book includes a cookbook with recipes that drivers may enjoy while living on the road and cooking on-board, with the hopes it may save the driver some money and eat healthy, while out on the road.

Again, the views and opinions written are the viewpoints of the author and in no way, has any outside organization influenced its content.

8

Have you ever, at some point in your life, driven down the interstate and seen a big shiny eighteen wheeler pass you; or driven late at night on a Thursday night and seen dozens of trucks coming down the highway in the distance and wondered what it would be like to be the commander of one of those vessels?

If you were fortunate to talk at length with one of the many professional truck drivers, you probably already know the ins and outs of the trucking industry. If you are related to a professional driver, you know firsthand the rewards and sacrifices that go with this type of job.

Many young people, fresh out of school and entering the workforce wonder at the wages a driver makes each year. They get excited at the concept of bringing home a big paycheck and entertain the notion of being able to experience the freedom afforded to a driver and seek to learn what it takes to become a fellow driver.

With no employment on the horizon and desperate, you scan the daily classified ads looking for anything that even hints of an interview and see columns of help wanted ads for drivers, amazed at the amount of pay promised each year. "Drivers Wanted". No experience necessary... free training...call this number for more information."

Excited at being able to return to the workforce, you pick up the phone and dial the number and begin talking to a recruiter who tells you about all the wonderful opportunities awaiting you at the nearest trucking school. The recruiter tells you about the biggest paycheck of your life and the offers you a free bus ticket to the school with free room and board. You are convinced and, knowing nothing more about trucking, hang up and pack what little possessions you own and head to the bus depot to embark what is sure to be a marvelous adventure.

It is not until you get to the school that you find out the ins and outs of the industry. You and the other hopefuls in your class do not find out what being a driver truly entails until you have spent some time behind the wheel with a seasoned trainer. Finally, it is not until you have graduated and are in your own truck, the realities of the trucking industry and all it entails sinks in.

The purpose of this book, as you will hear repeatedly, is to introduce you, the curious reader, to the world of trucking. It is also to provide a bit of entertainment to the professional driver and to finally do what others have talked and complained about for years.

You see, many drivers talk about how if they only knew what trucking really was; they would never have gotten into the field. The driver who truly loves his craft will always tell it the way it is because as lovers of the open road, we want to be out here and want to keep those who do not love the road, off of it.

If I recruit a reader of this book into the world of trucking, great! If I can prevent someone who realizes that trucking, after all, really would not be for him or her, then I've done my job. We all want peace out here and the last thing we want is a disillusioned driver out on the road with us with a chip on their shoulder because, as we hear many times, "I don't want to be here" or "They didn't tell me this or that". Well I am here to tell you that if you don't want to be out on the road, driving a semi truck, we will be the first to tell you that there are other jobs waiting for you elsewhere.

This book is not intended to discourage a person from pursuing trucking, however, it is intended to make you seriously examine all that becoming a driver entails so that you can make an informed decision about your career choice.

Now, if you are looking for a job, where you work eight hours a day, five days a week with weekends off, this is not the job for you. If you are looking for a job, where you can work twelve hours a day and have four days off each week, then this also is not the job for you. If you like being home every day (or night) and enjoy spending quality time with your families, this is definitely NOT the job for you. If you do not like to drive, hate driving in inclement weather, or like to stay indoors on cold, snowy days you need to look elsewhere.

Sorry. This must sound pretty discouraging by now, however if you are considering a lifestyle of the professional truck driver, the above job description does not apply here. It is better to find out now, before you leave your families and the comforts of your home.

You will spend several weeks learning how to drive a truck. Countless hours are spent learning how to read a map, use a logbook and learn to back a trailer between two straight lines. Not to mention driving the tractor without grinding all those gears.

You will learn how to do a proper pre-trip and post-trip inspection. You will also learn how to release excess water from the air brakes. This is especially important to know on a nice cold day so that when you are driving down a pretty mountain grade your brake lines don't freeze up and you can actually stop without using the side of the mountain as a buffer. Now is a good time to explain the differences between car brakes and semi-truck brakes.

Cars have hydraulic brakes. They normally stop whenever you apply pressure to the brake. You can press on them all day long and you still have brakes. If you apply pressure to the semi-trucks "air brakes", and you keep pressing down on those brakes without giving the air pressure time to rebuild...you will NOT have brakes...you will not be able to stop.

Good tip for the average car driver driving slow in front of a semi truck going down a grade. You can drive slow and brake all you want... the poor trucker behind you is sweating because you are forcing him to use his or her brakes more than they should and could cause a serious problem...like...NO BRAKES! And since we are on the subject of brakes, please note that it takes the length of a football field to stop a truck.

So please, take this into account the next time you cut in front of a truck in traffic. Safety is EVERYONE's responsibility, and it could save your life and the lives around you. I apologize for that previous rant but some of you might not get past this first chapter when you realize the job demands that is professional driving is not for you. Because of this realization, I threw this little public alert out to all of you in hopes of preventing a serious accident later on down the road. I think that everyone would agree that this is a huge problem on our highways.

Now, if you do not mind a flexible work schedule and do not mind being perpetually lost at all times, a career in trucking may be the choice for you. If you love the idea of not having someone standing behind you all day, telling you what to do all of the time, this is a career choice for you. If you love to travel, and drive to places you have been or have never been to, you will find trucking a great job. If you can manage your time, or learn to, and be flexible enough to change your plans often, this could be the right choice. If you have the patience to wait in line at the customer to load or unload, without causing yourself or your fellow drivers' grief about the wait time, this is the job for you. In the field of trucking, no day is the same and your experience at a customer may not always be the same each visit. Some days, you will arrive with your load on time, happy to see the customer and get in and out within thirty minutes. The next visit may take you up to four hours.

You have to understand that there are several drivers with similar loads from countless shippers with freight that needs to be unloaded. Sometimes, it is a first-come, first-serve basis. Most times, it is by appointment only and if you are even five minutes late, that five-minutes may cost you up to twenty-four hours in wait time. It depends on how many trucks are waiting, and the mood of the customer.

Oh, and just so you know many places are not very truck-friendly. They love to see you with their freight, but most will not let you park at their facilities. The Department of Transportation (D.O.T) is very strict on how many hours you can drive each day. At the moment, you are allowed to drive eleven hours a day. If you get to the customer and you are out of hours, you will be in a lot of trouble if you have no place to park for ten hours.

As most drivers will tell you, it is not just the customers who are not very truck friendly; there are some states that are lacking in truck parking. If you do not plan accordingly, you can find yourself in a lot of trouble. If you get caught, the fines could equal an entire weeks pay or more.

The fines that a driver can rack up depend on how a driver drives. If you speed, do not weigh your loads correctly, or violate the hours of service rules, amongst other things, it can be costly. If you are looking for a job where you do not get fined for doing things wrong, consider a different field. Trucking can get expensive if you are not careful. If you decide to become a professional driver and become careless and cause an accident, you basically just ended your career in trucking. If you roll a truck and trailer, you have just lost your job in most cases. If you falsify logbooks you can get a pretty stiff fine, and lose your job.

There is not much room for error out here folks. A small error can cost millions of dollars in lost freight, and can cost lives that you just can't put a price tag on. The person you injure or kill due to your carelessness has loved ones. Remember that when you start the engine. It could be your own family one day.

In the two years that I have been driving, I have seen a lot of accidents. Some of the accidents I have seen were from drivers, truck and car, driving too fast or driving too tired. Please, if you are tired, pull over. I know the freight has to get there, but you do too. If you fall asleep at the wheel, everyone around you is at risk. Just slow down, be careful and stay awake.

To those I have not completely scared off, the following chapters talk about experiences on the road, great places to visit and the dreaded weigh station. To those who have decided that trucking is not for you after all, keep reading anyways. There are some great places in our great country you might want to visit and some funny stories you will miss if you close this book!

Chapter Two

Welcome to trucking 101, where I will share with you some insights of the world that is truck driving school. Some of you may have already contacted a recruiter at the various companies out there. Some of you already signed up and are just waiting to board a bus that will take you to the first day of the rest of your life. Here is a tip. You signed up for truck driving school, not the military.

If you decide that you do NOT want to do this, you are more than free to change your mind. Folks, I kid you not, but I actually had a woman show up at my room, in tears because she did NOT want to be there. This woman literally stood in the middle of our hotel room and whined for ten minutes on how she did not want to be there. I enlightened her. I said, "Ma'am, you be sure to tell them in the morning that you want to go home and they will be more than happy to send you home." The woman thought she was stuck there for the 21 days of training. No trucking company wants to spend hundreds of dollars training a student who does not really want to be a driver. Believe me; they spend the first three days thinking of ways to send you home!

The trucking companies (or at least the one I went to) do not ask for a physician statement, or do a drug test, or a comprehensive background check until you have arrived at the school. The first day of driving school is spent in orientation where they do a medical physical and drug screen test. They do a background check at least twenty years, depending on the company. The trucking companies have to comply with D.O.T regulations and you are subject to all kinds of rules and regulations.

Now would be a good time to let you know that being a professional driver is not just about driving. You are responsible to paperwork, permits and all laws and regulations for each and every state you drive through. You will learn about Hazmat, IFTA registration, alcohol permits and more. The rules change and your job is to keep up. The first day of driving school is not the only time you will be getting a drug test. You are subject to random drug testing. My husband, who team drives with me, got pulled in three times for a drug screen and alcohol test. If you get selected multiple times, it is not that the company has you on their hit list. It is the luck of the draw and the list is selected by the D.O.T. and not the company.

The first week of driving school is spent in a classroom setting where you prepare to take your written exam. You have to pass this exam in order to receive a permit to learn to drive. In other words, you don't get past go without passing the exam. There are free, online programs out there that have prep test questions to prepare you for the exam. It would be worth your while to check out these sites as a study guide. Oh, and another friendly tip. They do check for warrants at the department of public safety.

The driving school I attended warned us from day one about this. They even put up a phone number to call to check if your social security number listed any outstanding warrants. On the day of the written exam, there were actually people who did not get off the bus. When the instructor asked them what the problem was, he was told that they did not think they should go in because they had outstanding warrants. They spent the whole week; wasted, knowing they could not go inside that building. The instructor got quite a chuckle over that one and when he told us the following day, so did we.

The second week of driving school comprised of what was called the range. This was where we learned how to back a tractor trailer. Looking back, oh man was I horrible. I couldn't back a trailer in a straight line to save my life. If you are ever bored and want some free entertainment, just go find a driving school and watch the students straight line back...you won't be disappointed. Now some of you may get offended by what I just said but just remember. No driver was born with a steering wheel in their hands and no one is a perfect driver. Have fun with what you do and it will never be work. If you can't laugh at yourself you have no right laughing at others.

The rest of the time in school is spent out on the road. The instructor's goal is to get you to pass your road test. This is very important. The goal of these schools is not to make you good drivers. Their goal is to get you to pass your road test so you can get your CDL's. The six weeks after driving school is spent learning to polish what you have learned. You spend those weeks with an experienced driver. One thing you need to know ahead of time. Depending on the school you go to, you are put up in some sort of lodging and usually get some meals included. The hotel I stayed at had free breakfast and I got a $25 gift card each week to buy groceries. There was a microwave in my room.

Once you complete driving school you then attend orientation where you work for a trucking company. I know of at least one student who had to wait a week for a mentor. The company does not pay for meals if you are between orientation and getting assigned to a truck. Make sure that if you go to orientation and you have to wait for a mentor, bring some supplies with you. You will be very hungry after a few days. Even if it is just peanut butter and jelly, or rice cakes...something that you can snack on. You need to eat.

If you make it to being assigned to a mentor, give yourself a pat on the back. Learning to drive a truck is not easy. It is one of the hardest things I ever did and one of the most exhilarating moments of my life was when I earned my CDL and passed the six week training.

Great, you have passed driving school, tested into a truck of your own and you are ready to strike out on your own. Are you prepared? Do you have the necessities that are needed while on the road for a week or two on the road? Now, let me explain the difference between necessities and luxuries. Necessities are the basic essentials that you are going to need. I recommend you get them as soon as possible, if not right away. It depends on your budget and on what you can afford right away. The number one thing is a CB radio. If your company does not issue you a CB, you really must have one. You can start out with a cheap one. I just saw them at Walmart for $39 and that was for a basic one. If you have to beg or borrow (don't steal!) to get one right away, get it. The hazards on the highway could be known ahead of time if you have a CB, and actually have it turned it ON.

Now, this is a sincere plea to my fellow drivers out there. I know that sometimes life on the road can be difficult and lonely and even a little bit depressing. If you are a solo driver, you are alone with your thoughts for hours at a time. If you don't like yourself much, be warned. You are going to be alone with yourself for a very long time. If you are a team and driving with a spouse like I am, you are both going to be together in close quarters for a very long time. If you get into an argument, I admit that you can't slam that curtain hard enough. But you have to like each other and get along well. If you do not get along outside of the truck, what makes you think you'll get along in small quarters?

It's just something to think about. Back to my plea...please tune it down on the CB. It is a long road out there and while we are trying to raise public awareness about how professional we are, we need to be able to prove it in all aspects of our lives and it is not very convincing if the powers that be, were to turn on the CB and listen to five minutes of what is spewed on that CB. It may make you feel better to get it off your chests and may reduce stress, but CB's are family oriented and there may be kids tuning in.

Remember, drivers need to have the CB on in the event of an accident, construction or something ahead that could potentially cause havoc on the road. We need to be able to hear that warning come across, so the "if you don't like what is being said, turn it off" attitude really doesn't work in this case. Again, it may be your family in that accident up ahead and I am sure you would not want it made worse by having a fellow trucker, who did not hear about an accident and a back-up on the highway, drive into the accident because they couldn't stop in time. This example is a real scenario. A driver did not have their CB on. The driver was going at 55 mph around a curb and did not know traffic was stopped on the other side of the curb. I will leave it to the reader's imagination the result of that scenario.

If you are a brand new driver and cannot afford a CB right away, drive carefully and treat every curve as if there is something on the other side. You should do that anyway. It takes seconds for a truck to roll over and if you aren't careful and expecting the worse, you will not be able to stop if a truck rolls in front of you.

The only other thing you need to have on board are some warm blankets or a sleeping bag, warm clothing, a hat and gloves during the winter months. Make sure you have chains on board your truck if you are driving in the snow. Chains are good not only in the mountains but also on flat terrain. A driver was in New Mexico where it snowed and the highways were shut down. Ice formed in the parking lots and the driver got stuck. He could not get out of his parking spot. If he'd had chains on board, he might have been able to throw them on, and possibly could have gotten out.

My husband and I went to a customer in Chicago to pick up a loaded trailer. It had snowed and the lot was icy. Another driver was there and couldn't get the trailer out. All we had on board that we thought might provide some traction was a box of minute rice. Luckily, it worked. The driver got out and the birds got fed well that day! Make sure you have food on board in case of road closures and you are stuck out in the middle of nowhere for a few hours or days. Snow storms have a funny way of shutting down highways and you want to make sure you have a few days worth of food or you are going to be miserable, hungry and eventually sick.

Truck stops are a great place to go for food, rest, and relaxation. You have an opportunity to talk to other drivers. Just one word of caution... expensive! It is expensive to eat at a truck stop for each and every meal, day in and day out. Laundry facilities are more costly. You are paying for the convenience. While it can be expensive to frequent a truck stop, please support them. There are very few places that allow trucks and it is expensive to run a truck stop. Please keep this in mind. It may cost a few extra dollars but they are there for us, for the most part. One place you can normally park your truck without too much hassle is a Walmart. Most Walmart's are truck-friendly. Some are not. Here is another plea to our fellow drivers. Please do not throw your trash out onto Walmart's parking lot. It makes them not want us to be there anymore and it is one of the few places we can go to rest and shop for groceries without us being asked to leave. You can get a good cooler (igloo, Coleman) to put on board and fill it with perishables.

Contrary to popular opinion, you can eat healthy out here if you plan your trips right. My husband and I buy salad mix, fruits and vegetables that fit well into those coolers. Milk, juice and water also do nicely for a few days. You can buy a full sized Crockpot and cook on board with it if you have an inverter. It works best on the lower two speeds. High does not work well, but you can cook a good, healthy meal on low and warm. Some of the meals we cooked were roasts, chicken, eggplant parmesan, and pork chop. We have cooked smoked sausage and sauerkraut. All of the truck stops sell 12 volt appliances such as coffee pots, lunchbox stoves, water heaters and more. We have actually cooked Pillsbury grands biscuits in that lunchbox stove. It also cooks chicken, soups and other foods rather well. You just need to turn the food now and then to even cook the food and prevent it from burning. This book includes some recipes that we have found that work well. This will be in the last section of this book.

Before I move on to fun stories, and names and places, I have one more word of advice where truck stops are concerned. The truck moves, not the road. You get paid by the mile, not the hour. If you drive from truck stop to truck stop, you will not make any money out here. Every time you stop, for whatever reason; even if it is just to use the restroom, you have lost a minimum of thirty minutes. It takes thirty minutes to slow the truck down to a stop, park, and do whatever you need to do and get back out and back to speed. If you stop to eat, you have lost an hour.

You have just gotten a glimpse of what trucker life is like. If you are still interested, hurry up and get out here. We need your help! If you got this far and you are still skeptical, this is the real deal. This is what life is like, in my opinion. As a team driver, I have the opportunity to drive with my spouse. I always have someone to talk to and we really enjoy driving. While it may not be for everyone, driving can be very rewarding. My husband and I have gotten to see some beautiful places. If not for driving, we would never have seen most of these places. But it is your choice, not mine. Good luck with your decision!

Chapter Three

Okay, let's have some fun. Here is a little game of trivia to help you pass the time and test your brain. The answers to these questions can be found at the end of the chapter.

1. On what highway, and what state is Donner Pass located?

2. On what highway is Black Mountain located and what is the speed limit for this grade?

3. What states does Interstate 40 run through?

4. Hurricane is located in what state?

5. What is the speed limit for trucks in Illinois?

6. What is the name of the Rest Area on interstate 40 when you first come into Arizona, coming from New Mexico?

7. Where is Truckee located?

8. In what state is White Sands located?

9. At what exit, is the BMW plant, in Greer, SC?

10. The Iowa 80 Truck stop is located in what state and on what highway?

11. How many hours does it take to get from one end of Los Angeles to the other during rush hour on a Friday night?

12. Devils Peak is located in what state?

13. What is the name of the trucker channel on Sirius Radio?

14. In what state and what highway is "the gorge" located?

15. What is the required speed limit through "the gorge"?

16. What is the highway off of interstate 10, in Arizona that goes to San Diego?

17. Do the toll roads in Oklahoma and Kansas or Ohio allow EZ pass?

18. What state does NOT recognize Prepass?

19. Give one reason why you love your job.

20. What are all trucks required to do, if open, when they enter a state?

(See page 105 for the answers)

Chapter Four

There is nothing like driving down the highway on a cool summer day, through the winding mountains of Wyoming on interstate 80. It is even more impressive to see the white-capped mountains on interstate 70 from Denver to Vale, Colorado. The drive through the mountainous canyons and mountain peaks of Utah, on any highway is breathtaking. Flagstaff, Arizona has a beauty that is insurmountable. The state of California is breathless as you make your way very slowly, at 55 mph from Needles to Barstow. California is gorgeous from San Diego to Sacramento with its winding roads and peaks and breathtaking valleys. Black Mountain, in North Carolina going East Bound has some beautiful views. The view is beautiful but its descent can be deadly if you aren't careful. I named it Cowabunga hill! The most beautiful stretch of road I have seen is on interstate 80, through Truckee and Donner's Pass, in California. Our great country has vast beauty. Appreciate that we are free to enjoy it!

One of the most beautiful stretches of road is Highway 50 Westbound out of Pueblo, Colorado. If you have some time and are not in a hurry, this stretch is for you! There are some Kodak moments in this stretch of switchbacks that open into some of the most breathtaking views you'll ever see. There are few places where you can park your truck but there are pullouts before just about every town on the way.

Each road has its own uniqueness and every driver has his or her own favorite stretch of highway. Beauty is in the eye of the beholder, and what is great for me is certainly different for another. For this reason, I can only describe the many roads I've traveled. In a subsequent book I will be illustrating by state, various landmarks and favorite spots that can be viewed on the road, as well as truck-friendly establishments who are there for your convenience.

Chapter Five

Life on the highway is full of beauty and wonder. As a driver, we also encounter frustration and discouragement. We need to find humor in those awkward moments when we encounter not so very humorous things. As a new driver, my moments of awkwardness came from the dreaded weigh stations. Not very experienced, I found myself in embarrassing moments and at odds with the weigh master. I have since found much humor in those early days of my driving career. The first such incident occurred on Hwy 84 in Oregon.

The great state of Oregon has a sense of humor also. They decided to put a weigh station in the middle of a steep grade. Oh what fun that was! Now, let me explain this from my point of view. I had been driving through states with my mentor, who was also my spouse, and so he did most of the driving during which time HE drove through the weigh stations. So I had little experience. I also noticed that most of the weigh stations he drove through had a posted speed limit of 30 mph.

So here I am, driving through Oregon's weigh station. I saw the 3. In my mind though, the speed limit was 30 as I was accustomed. It was 3 mph. I had to stop, back up, and try again. Then I got to take all of my paperwork into the weigh station and say hello to the nice weigh master. Oh what fun that was. He asked to see my Oregon permit. I had a permit book in my hands but I never really looked through it. I of course, looked confused so the weigh master looked through the book for me. Then he asked to see my driver license. He then told me that he could tell that I was so obviously new, that he would let me off with a warning. He must have noticed my look of confusion because he then said…"because you do not have an Oregon permit". I asked him if it was not in the permit book. He then opened the book to the page where an Oregon permit ought to be. In its place was a notice that said, "Please contact the permit department at least one hour prior to entry". I looked at the weigh master with an incredulous look and asked him why they would even do that? I mean, if they are going to waste paper, why not just put a permit there? The weigh master let me go and I think the reason is because he couldn't keep a straight face anymore. He was laughing hysterically by the time I got to the door.

So the next time you encounter a similar situation, try to find some humor in it, and learn from your mistakes. We are, after all, human.

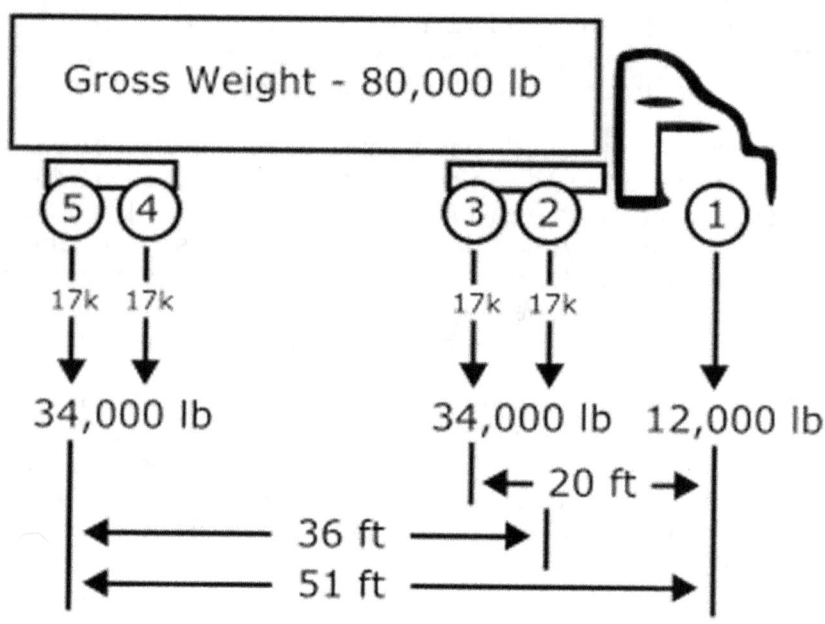

Chapter Six

Okay, if you made it this far, it is obvious that you are serious about a career in the trucking industry. Congratulations on your decision and rest assured you are in good company. There are many drivers out here who really love their jobs and despite what you might hear on the CB radio or in the truck stop, or anywhere else truckers like to congregate, trucking is not that bad of an endeavor.

As I stated once before, no one out here is forced to be out here and there are other jobs if you decide you absolutely hate the trucker life. I have spent much time on the negative aspects of trucking and with good reason. Trucking is not for everyone and I want to be very clear that it can be lonely and costly in many aspects. On the other hand, trucking can be very rewarding and fulfilling.

The trucking industry has one of the highest turn-over rates overall and every company advertises that their pay package and home time is the best option. For this reason, many drivers leave their respective trucking companies to see if the grass is greener in someone else's yard. Let me explain something here. Yes, some companies pay a cent or two more for experience but you need to look at the big picture. If you switch companies for a penny raise, make sure you aren't paying elsewhere. Some companies reimburse for showers while others do not. Some companies reimburse for tolls but only if they are pre-authorized. Not every company has pre-pass or EZ pass. Also, if you switch companies, your seniority just went away.

You have to earn the trust of new dispatchers and you have to learn the habits of a new driver manager. Also, you have to wait to get benefits. Most companies will only vest 100% 401K after five years of service. I am not saying that switching isn't a wise choice. Just make sure that when you switch companies that you understand all that it entails. When you are young and just starting out, switching jobs won't mean much to you. It is a whole new ballgame when you are in your forties and you haven't invested in your retirement and then expect a company to match your retirement plan. It is a two-way street with most companies. They want your loyalty in exchange for theirs.

Retirement is very important. When you retire, you need to make sure you can afford to and that you have spent the previous year's saving. Remember, your bills will not go down much and your rent and cost of living expenses won't go away.

Chapter Seven

There are great advantages of being a truck driver. If you have previous customer service skills and have worked in an office setting, you have the option of working as a driver manager or other office professional in the trucking industry.

Working as a truck driver gives you the skills and understanding of what a driver goes through on a day to day basis. If you work in an office environment and have never driven a big rig before, you have no clue what a driver goes through. You don't know how lonely it may get out there, or how long it took a driver to get through Columbus, Ohio during a morning rush hour.

You have never experienced sitting in traffic for three hours because both sides of the freeway are shut down because a semi rolled over five miles ahead of you. You never thanked God because it was another driver who rolled over, or another driver whose cab is on fire, or that you hit a car that cut in front of you and not knowing if that person survived.

An office person who picks up the phone and wants to go home because they only come in to work a forty hour work week can't understand why the driver wants to talk about nothing work-related for ten minutes because they have no one else to talk to.

A late night dispatcher doesn't want to talk to a driver about a load he or she needs to get home because his or her kid is sick. A driver is out on the road for weeks at a time and just because someone at home needs them, doesn't mean the company is going to be able to get that driver home on time. If there is no freight going close to their home, that driver isn't getting there. In spite of all of this knowledge, many drivers still love their jobs. They love the freedom that is driving. They love the idea that they wake up in one state and go to sleep later that night in some other state. They love the challenge of finding the customer and getting freight delivered on time.

The last two sections of this book will be devoted to a few recipes that my husband and I used while driving, and a sample diary of the day to day life on the road.

Again, I am not endorsing any particular brand of food. The sole purpose of this section is to give you an idea of what you can cook and keep your costs down while out on the road. Your own preferences and tastes will overrule any ideas I give you.

Chapter Eight

Just about anything you can pick up in a grocery store will work well in a crock pot or stove. If you go to the freezer section of the supermarket, you will find complete crock pot meals that will keep nicely in a cooler for a few days. The only thing I found that did not cook well was pasta. However, there is a pasta maker out there that you can buy. From what I hear from other drivers, this pasta maker works great and makes great spaghetti, though I have not tried it myself. I have made roasts, chicken, pot roast, soup...you name it, and I have pretty much tried it. One thing though...if you are trying to cook a large piece of meat, it may take several hours to cook it. You may want to start your dinner the night before if you want to eat it when you are ready for it. If you use the stove, be aware that food cooks much faster and you want to check your food frequently to keep it from burning.

Try this:

Option 1

1 box of herb stuffing

2 chicken breasts (skinless)

1 can mixed vegetables

Prepare the stuffing as you would at home. Moisten stuffing and put a layer on the bottom of crock pot. Lay the chicken breast on top of the stuffing. Cover chicken with remaining stuffing so that entire chicken is covered. Cook on medium until done. About fifteen minutes before you are ready to eat, open can of mixed vegetables (drained) and pour on top of chicken and stuffing. This provides a tasty and healthy meal.

Option 2

If you are able to get to a Walmart or grocery store where you can park your rig, here is another tasty treat that, when made right, can feed you for a few days:

1 fully cooked roast chicken from deli counter

1 small container of mustard potato salad

1 small jar of jalapeno

1 avocado

1 small container of sour cream

1 package of corn tostadas

Pull pieces of chicken off of the bones and mix it with the mustard potato salad. Add jalapenos to taste and add 2 tablespoons of sour cream. If you choose to add an avocado, be sure it is very ripe as you want to blend it with the potato salad. Take spoonfuls of mixture and put it on a tostada. This makes a lot and you can store it in your cooler for the next day's lunch. This is easy to make and no cooking is required. You can eat it with the chicken still warm or chilled.

Option 3:

1 package of Kielbasa (or smoked sausage)

1 jar or can of sour kraut

Cut kielbasa or sausage in bite sized pieces and put into crock pot. Add sour kraut and let cook on medium. Watch the time on this because it cooks fast and will dry out or burn quickly.

You may prefer the fresh sour kraut that is usually found in the meat department where kielbasa or hot dogs are sold. Unless you have containers for the excess, rethink this. It has been my experience that it spills or leaks easily and nothing is worse than the juice pooling on the bottom of the cooler. It makes a mess!

Option 4

Go to the freezer section and pick out chicken patties, veggie patties, or just about any type of pre-cooked cutlet-type food of your choice.

Add a scoop of rice (do not use minute rice for this meal as the rest of the food in this dish will not cook as quickly).

Add a can of vegetables of your choosing (do NOT drain water)

The water in the vegetables will cook the rice.

Place the patty on top of the rice and vegetables

It takes about an hour to cook. Keep in mind that cook time varies and you want to check in the beginning how long it takes for these meals to cook.

If you pour water into the cooking tins of the stove, add a couple of eggs and plug the stove into the cigarette lighter. You can have hard boiled eggs on hand for a quick meal or make yourself an egg salad sandwich.

These are just a few of many options you have. The sky is the limit and you only need to experiment to see what works

The small bread-tins fit the stove well and can be gotten cheaply at Walmart or other store of your choice.

Get a Crockpot. Crockpot liners can be found at Walmart, which makes for easy clean-up. This is especially convenient out on the road.

It is very easy to prepare food for the next day by using a crock pot. Examples of meals we have made out of a Crockpot:

Pot Roast-add potatoes and vegetables no more than 2-3 hours before you are ready to eat the meal or it will get mushy.

Chicken-again, add vegetables when chicken is close to being completely cooked or it will get mushy.

Soups-whether it is from left over chicken or out of the can, it is very easy to heat soups in this manner.

If you like eggplant, it cooks nicely in the crock pot.

1 small eggplant

1 can hunts spaghetti sauce (or whatever brand you like)

1 small bag of shredded mozzarella cheese

Mushrooms (optional)

Green pepper (optional, diced)

Slice the eggplant and layer it with the cheese and sauce mixed with mushrooms and green pepper and cook on medium until eggplant is tender.

The possibilities are endless. There are packages of Crockpot meals in the freezer section of most grocers. Just follow the directions.

Microwaves:

If your company allows inverters to be placed in the trucks, a microwave is a great way of eating on the road. There are hundreds of foods that can be cooked. However, many companies do NOT allow inverters so be sure to check their policy before purchasing one.

You should stock up on canned foods and I highly recommend them because there is only so much room in that cooler. Also, if you are stuck at a customer or you have not had time to restock, having extra canned foods will be handy. Sandwiches are easy to make. A jar of peanut butter and a jar of jelly make for a quick meal. A few cans of tuna fish would also be a great healthy choice.

Lunch meats can be purchased and keep for several days and make for quick meals. Fresh fruits and vegetables keep very well for several days.

It is very important that you understand what I am about to tell you. You MUST keep a couple of day's worth of food on board your truck. You never know when an emergency will come up. You can spend hours or days in a place where there is no place to get food.

If you get stranded on Interstate 80 in Pennsylvania due to a blizzard that shuts down the highway, trust me when I say there are no restaurants in walking distance. The same applies to Wyoming, Colorado, and New Mexico.

It would be very courteous to keep extra supplies on hand in case a fellow driver gets caught without food or water. The driver you help out there may very well be the driver who helps you if you find yourself in compromising situations.

Chapter Nine

Keep in mind that you will be spending a large amount of your time driving that truck. You will need to adjust your caloric intake, depending on how much exercise you fit into your routine.

Becoming a Professional Driver can be a very unhealthy proposition if you don't take care of yourself. Diabetes and Sleep Apnea are only a few of an assortment of disorders that plague the trucking industry. It is important that you watch what you eat, exercise, and get plenty of rest.

Proper Hygiene is important. Nobody wants to see a driver who looks like he or she just rolled out of bed. There is NO excuse why you cannot stop at a truck stop and take a shower. If you don't have time to stop and shower before you go to the shipper and again before you reach the consignee, you don't have time to take the load!

The following are some tips to consider:

Exercise:

Park your truck as far as possible from the truck stop entrance and walk. It is great exercise and helps to increase your circulation. Blood pools into your buttocks area and thighs and can cause blood clots if you are not moving around. To prevent this, you want to stop at least every three hours and walk around. This would also give you the opportunity to do a walk around and inspect your equipment.

If you are parked at a truck stop or rest area, spend at least thirty minutes walking around the parking lot. Of course, you want to do this in a well-lit area. Meet your fellow drivers out there and invite them to join you. Safety increases in numbers!

Carry a jump rope in your truck and use it. It is a cheap and easy way to work out.

I have seen some drivers carry bicycles on their trucks. This is a great way to exercise and visit the area you are in. This is especially true if there are lakes or parks nearby with bike trails. Believe it or not, there is a shipper in Chicago that has such a park right across the street. They have bike and/or walking trails. There are also picnic areas here so you can bike it and then make a picnic of it. This is great if the shipper is going to be hours before getting you loaded.

The steps on the truck are great stretching machines! Walking around the truck several times will allow you to walk while keeping your equipment in sight if you have a high-value load.

These are just a few ideas. I am sure you can think of your own as well!

Hygiene is very important. If you find yourself waiting a day or two for a load and are able to stay at a hotel, be sure to check out that hotel. There are some very nice hotels out there for reasonable rates. Most of them have CDL discounts. If you have an AARP membership, there are substantial savings available to you as well.

You are bound to come across a hotel that looks a bit shady. If in doubt, look somewhere else. You have no idea who was in that room before you and if the room looks disgusting, then it is! Ask to inspect the room before you check in. Bed bugs and lice can be horrible experiences out on the road. It doesn't happen often, but it CAN happen. Be prepared. A bottle of lice-killing shampoo is not out of order. Hydro-cortisone creams are great items to carry with you. Don't put yourself in a bad situation. Choose a reputable hotel. Many even allow pets for an extra fee. Hotel guides can be found at most rest areas.

Showers at truck stops are usually clean and in good repair. There are, however some horrible truck stops out there. You will come across these and will make a point not to revisit them!

Chapter Ten

This section illustrates a day to day diary of life on the road. Due to the times we face in a tough economic environment, I must confess that this diary may seem to be biased since it covers a short period of time which cannot be compared to the same time in subsequent years. Also, let me point out that each driver differs in their day to day activities so my experiences may be different than another drivers.

The biggest difference that I can point out is that of the Company Driver and the Owner Operator. My husband and I both worked as Company Drivers for several years before leasing on with our company. We have been Lease Owner Operators for over a year now. A year ago, we ran teams and averaged five to six thousand miles a week. In today's freight environment, we are averaging 3 to 4 thousand miles a week. Some weeks, we average less, depending on where we are in the country and whether or not we decided to take a day or two off that week.

We, like most drivers, get paid by the mile. As owner operators, we do not get layover pay. We are responsible for paying our own taxes and obtaining are own health insurance coverage. We pay our own fuel expenses. Our truck payment and added expenses is around $732 a week. Whether we run or not, we still have a truck payment and expenses to cover.

We put aside twenty-cents a mile to cover maintenance costs. If the truck breaks down, it is up to us to fix it. Replacing tires on our truck can range into over a thousand dollars. An oil change and inspection is more than three hundred dollars, which is needed every twenty-thousand miles. Twenty-thousand miles may seem like a long time but remember, we average three to four thousand miles a week, so we need to change the oil every 5 weeks or so.

To the average person, filling up a tank of fuel ranges anywhere from twenty-five to forty dollars. A semi-truck costs around four to five hundred dollars to fill up. On average, we fuel up every day. We drive on average, a thousand to twelve hundred miles per day. That is a lot of fuel each week and a large chunk of revenue lost each year.

There are additional expenses for gear that are a must in the trucking industry. During the winter months, a set of chains are not just common sense items, but legally required items in some states. California, Colorado and Nevada are some such examples. Chains are not only needed for climbing and descending steep terrain, but can also help provide traction on icy surfaces in truck stops. Many drivers would have loved to have a set to get them out of icy parking spots. Believe it or not, a box of minute rice can also get you out of a bad spot...we've used this to help another driver get out of a space.

Rubbing alcohol, gloves, boots, warm clothing and non-perishable foods are a must have on board the truck. There should also be a first aid kit on board. Extra blankets or a good sleeping bag will help out should you ever break down and are not able to run the engine.

In inclement weather, be prepared for highway closures in both the northern and southern part of the country. Believe it or not, the southern states get bad weather and have road closures just as often as those in the north. This information is crucial because many drivers have been caught unawares on the road, with no supplies. You can be shut down for days. Interstate 40 in New Mexico and Arizona have been notorious for highway closures. Flagstaff Arizona is at a higher elevation and is famous for snow and icy conditions. My sister and brother-in-law sat in New Mexico for three days waiting for the highways to reopen.

Two years ago, Interstate 10 in San Antonio Texas was shut down for hours due to icy road conditions. Interstate 70 in Vale Colorado is famous for shutdowns. The same can be said for interstates 25, 80 and 90. High Winds, Rain, Fog, Snow and Ice all can wreak havoc on a truck driver's day. Most people get to stay home from work or school on inclement days. Truck Drivers are still out on the roads and have to wait it out on the side of the road or rest area until the roads are cleared up. It is vital that the driver be prepared for these situations.

It may seem that there is repetition in this book, but there is no such thing as too much information where the truck driver is concerned. If you didn't get the hint in earlier chapters, then please take heed in this one. The road out there is no joke and many drivers lose their lives. I prefer to err on the side of caution. Many new drivers have no clue as to what to expect. Many do not even have a CB radio to warn them of dangerous conditions ahead of them. I must urge you right now, if you do not have a CB radio installed in your truck to please get one. There are obstacles in the road as you drive and the safe driver is the informed one. If there is an accident ahead, or a power line in the road, you can get notified, or notify your fellow drivers if you happen on it first. Many shippers communicate with drivers via the CB radio. Weigh Stations are equipped with CB radios and if you ever have a problem out there on the road, the Weigh Master can be your friend. Also, Law enforcement Officials has CB radios and can be helpful to the driver in most instances.

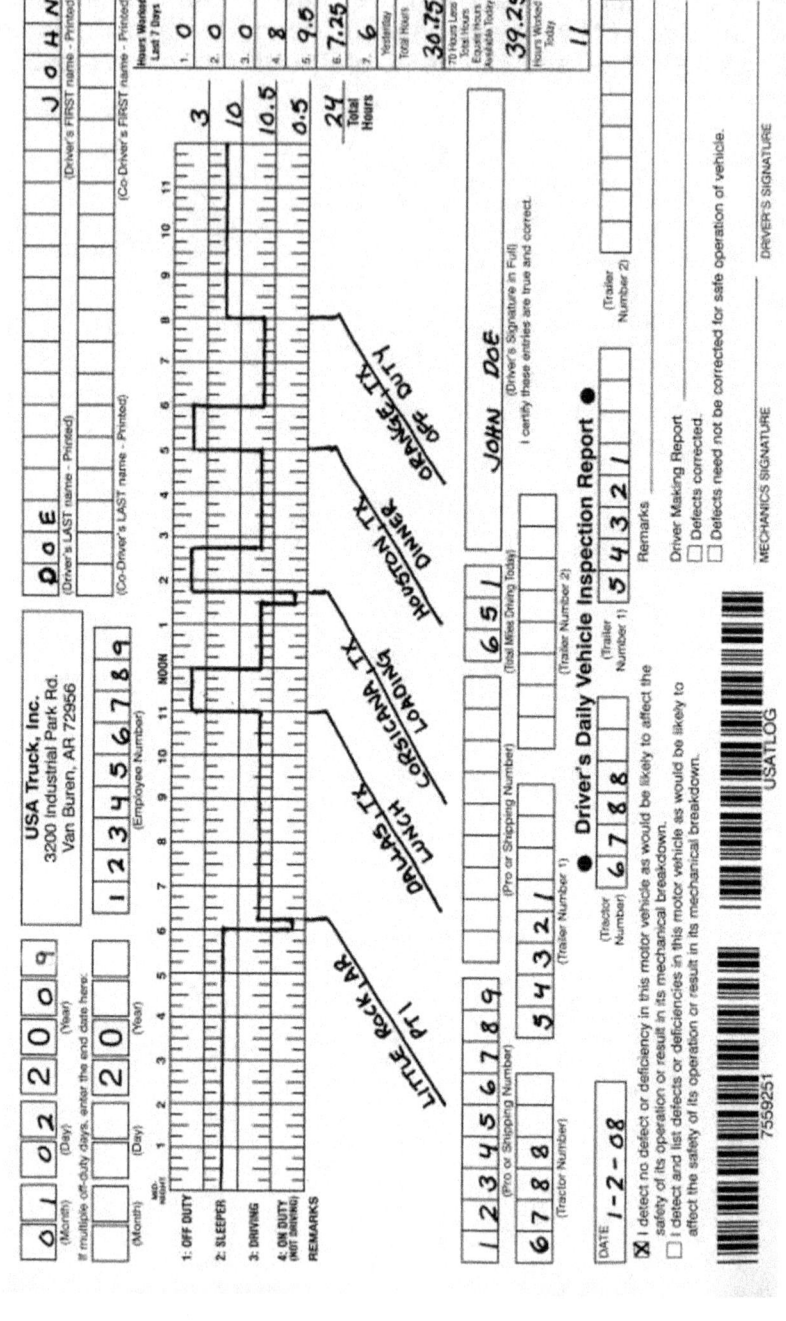

USA Truck, Inc.
3200 Industrial Park Rd.
Van Buren, AR 72956

(Month) 0 1 (Day) 0 2 (Year) 2 0 0 9

If multiple off-duty days, enter the end date here.
(Month) 2 0 (Day) (Year)

(Employee Number) 1 2 3 4 5 6 7 8 9

Driver's LAST name - Printed: D O E
Driver's FIRST name - Printed: J O H N
(Co-Driver's LAST name - Printed)
(Co-Driver's FIRST name - Printed)

	MID-NIGHT	1	2	3	4	5	6	7	8	9	10	11	NOON	1	2	3	4	5	6	7	8	9	10	11	Total Hours
1: OFF DUTY																									3
2: SLEEPER																									10
3: DRIVING																									10.5
4: ON DUTY (NOT DRIVING)																									0.5
REMARKS																									24 Total Hours

REMARKS: LITTLE ROCK AR, DALLAS TX LUNCH, CORSICANA TX LOADING, HOUSTON TX DINNER, ORANGE TX OFF DUTY

Hours Worked Last 7 Days
1. 0
2. 0
3. 0
4. 8
5. 9.5
6. 7.25
7. 6 Yesterday

Total Hours 30.75

70 Hours Less Total Hours Equals Hours Available Today 39.25

Hours Worked Today 11

JOHN DOE (Driver's Signature in Full)
I certify these entries are true and correct.

(Pro or Shipping Number) 1 2 3 4 5 6 7 8 9
(Pro or Shipping Number) 6 7 8 8
(Trailer Number 1) 5 4 3 2 1
(Total Miles Driving Today) 6 5 1
(Trailer Number 2)

● Driver's Daily Vehicle Inspection Report ●

(Tractor Number) 6 7 8 8
(Trailer Number 1) 5 4 3 2 1
(Trailer Number 2)

Remarks

DATE 1-2-08

☒ I detect no defect or deficiency in this motor vehicle as would be likely to affect the safety of its operation or result in its mechanical breakdown.
☐ I detect and list defects or deficiencies in this motor vehicle as would be likely to affect the safety of its operation or result in its mechanical breakdown.

Driver Making Report
☐ Defects corrected.
☐ Defects need not be corrected for safe operation of vehicle.

_____
MECHANICS SIGNATURE

_____
DRIVER'S SIGNATURE

USATLOG

7559251

Chapter 11

This chapter outlines the log book and excerpts from my personal journal, in general form. It does not give a complete minute by minute accounting of our activities, but is meant to give the reader a general idea of how a team operates.

July 1, 2009

Having picked up a load in Albany Georgia, we are in route to Golden Colorado to deliver a load.

0145-0215: Georgia, Interstate 75 exit 298, Fuel Stop

0415: Tennessee, Interstate 24 exit 134, Post Trip Inspection. Go to sleeper

1730: Missouri, Interstate 70, exit 203, Pre Trip Inspection.

2145: Missouri, Interstate 70, exit 28, Stop for break

July 2, 2009

0100: Kansas, Interstate 70, exit 308, Post Trip Inspection, go to sleeper

1700: Colorado, Interstate 70, exit 278, dinner

2000: Golden Colorado, made delivery and picked up next load and in route to Elkton Virginia.

2330: Colorado, Interstate 70, exit 383, break

July 3, 2009

0100-0115: Kansas, Interstate 70, exit 6, break

0345: Kansas, Interstate 70, exit 145, Post Trip Inspection

1515-1700: Missouri, Interstate 70, exit 203, Out of truck with husband. Dinner, relaxation

1700: Pre Trip Inspection

1845: Illinois, Interstate 64, exit 25, break

2000-2145: Illinois, Mt. Vernon, Interstate 64, exit 95, Out of truck to do some shopping and grab dinner. (Walmart across street from truck stop)

July 4, 2009

0200: Kentucky, Interstate 64, exit 28, Post Trip Inspection, Go to sleeper

1730-1815: Virginia, Interstate 81, exit 235, Out of Truck for showers, dinner with husband, then return to sleeper and await next load assignment.

July 5, 2009

We are routed to Richmond Virginia to pick up our next load, which we are taking to Arlington Texas.

1330: Pre Trip Inspection

2000-2030: Virginia, Interstate 81, exit 77, break

2200-2215: Tennessee, Interstate 81, exit 74, break

2330-2345: Tennessee, Interstate 81, exit 4, break

July 6, 2009

0145: Tennessee, Interstate 40, exit 327, Post Trip Inspection, Go to sleeper

1230: Arkansas, Interstate 40, exit 221, Pre Trip Inspection

1330-1400: Arkansas, Interstate 40, exit 194, dinner break with husband

1630-1645: Arkansas, Interstate 30, exit 44, break

2100-2230: Texas, Interstate 20, exit 472, Out of Truck

2300: At customer and waiting to deliver in Arlington Texas.

This journal is general and meant to introduce a potential driver to the rigors that is the life of the truck driver. Unlike a routine 9-5 job, where you punch a time clock and put in your time and go home and have nothing to worry about until you return to work the next day, the routine of the truck driver is very different.

Look at the journal and take notice of the times. The first thing you should notice is that while the first few days, I was able to start driving at around 5pm each day, that one of those days I began my day at just past noon. Also notice the amount of time I spend driving. The time spent at a shipper, or a truck stop is different as well and noted as such.

A truck driver must account for every moment while out on the road, as well as while out of the truck. Time is separated into four distinct categories. All time spent inside the truck must be accounted for. A log book is used to keep track of this time. The time spent in the sleeper is noted on line 2. A driver must spend at least eight hours in the sleeper. While a driver is required to take a ten hour break, at least eight of those hours must be spent in the sleeper. The other two may be spent on line one to allow a driver to eat a meal, shower, do laundry or shop, or whatever is needed to be done.

If the driver is not required to stay with a load, or is waiting for the next load, then they can go to line 1. My husband and I use this line often since most times, we choose to stay in a hotel while waiting on a load. This is true especially if freight is slow and it may be a number of hours before our next load. Since we pay for our own fuel, it is actually cheaper for us to stay in a hotel than to idle the truck. Plus, we can take showers, watch television or go to the malls, or visit anything in the area.

All time spent driving must be put on line 3. If at a customer and unloading a truck or are required to remain with the load while it is being unloaded, or loaded, that time must be put on line 4 of the log book. This also includes time spent fueling as well as pre trips and post trips. It should be noted that a pre trip and post trip, respectively requires a notation of at least thirty minutes. Fueling can take anywhere from fifteen minutes to thirty minutes. Log books are done in fifteen minute increments. At the end of the day, all time is calculated. An over the road driver may only drive 70 hours a week, legally. We have to take a 34 hour break in order to reset the 70 hour clock.

It may seem confusing to absorb what is required while logging hours each day, but time and practice make it effortless. It is also legally required and there are some stiff penalties if you are caught without one. The penalties are even stiffer if it is found that you falsified your log book. It is federally mandated so do yourself a favor and just do it. One of the biggest benefits of maintaining a log book is the fact that everything in your life is pretty much documented. In the event of a mishap, that log book will prove useful in proving your innocence (or guilt).

Here is another example of what we do on a day to day basis:

Friday, October 2, 2009

We got to Conway Transportation an hour early. Our load picked up at 0300. It wasn't ready until 0430 and they were practically pushing us out of the parking lot. 'We can't push out the delivery time', they insisted. It was a hazmat load, though it had only 80 pounds on it. Still, we had to report the load to our company before we could depart.

We left Fontana and got onto interstate 15 and headed north. Clayton drove while I slept. The weather reports said all was clear in the northwest. I didn't believe that for a second. The weather changes by the minute and today was no exception. We had a little over a thousand miles to drive and less than 24 hours to get there.

We were bound for Butte Montana. I woke up in the early afternoon. I saw that we were just north of Las Vegas. I was starving. We didn't get a chance to get to the grocery store and so we had bare necessities on board. There weren't many options and we only had time to stop maybe two times maximum. We decided we could wait until we reached Cedar City Utah before stopping. It was a great place to fuel up and grabs a quick bite. We grabbed some extra sandwiches and some fruit for later. We walked Piper and headed back out on the road. There wasn't a cloud in the sky. It was in the sixties and we headed north again.

About this time I put the weather channel on again. It was my turn to drive so I wasn't very surprised to hear a change in the forecast. There was a disturbance in the northwest and it was headed towards the Montana and Idaho border. 'Perfect', I thought to myself. Luckily they said it wouldn't be until late Sunday until it arrived so I saw no problems with getting the load to Butte on time.

I kept headed north and was happy to get north of Salt Lake City. It was rush hour traffic and it went without a hitch. I noticed a lot of traffic going south and wondered at it. There had been no accidents or construction that I was able to tell so I put on the CB radio. One of the Universities was having a sporting event. 'Ah', I thought to myself. That explains it. I ran into some construction and there was an accident being cleared so the right lane was closed. I stayed in the center lane and maintained a safe following distance. As soon as the folks figured out that the right lane was closed, they would waste no time moving over and many didn't seem to think there was anyone around them. They just came over without a care in the world. Of course, the rest of us cared, but that is life on the road. I was happy that there were no further problems.

I made it to the Idaho border and was happy. This is one of my favorite states to drive through. It is gorgeous through here and I marveled at the view. Of course, it was beginning to get dark by the time I got half way across and was sad because I wouldn't have the view for much longer. I also noticed the temperatures dropping so I put the weather channel back on. There wasn't any change but I was noticing snow in the higher mountain elevations. I continued north into Montana.

Still, I couldn't help but worry about the weather. We had yet to get a load out of there and I didn't want to chance being stuck up there when the snow hit. I called the terminal and asked for a load out as soon as possible.

The temperatures fluctuated between the high twenties and low thirties. I made great time but by the time we made delivery, we hadn't heard a thing about another load, so we pulled over for the night and waited for morning.

Saturday, October 03, 2009

I woke up early and marveled at how awake and lively Clayton was. 'Let's go get some breakfast', he said. I asked him if we'd gotten a load yet and he said not yet. I sighed. Then he asked if I wanted to shower and do laundry while we were waiting. I laughed at him and said, 'Let me explain something to you. There is a snow storm headed this way. I'll eat breakfast and we can go take a shower but I want to get out of here as soon as possible.' He sighed and gave me a grin. He knows how I panic when there is snow and ice involved. We ate breakfast and showered and the showers at this truck stop were tiny to say the least, but at least they were clean. I took my shower first and then I waited in the TV lounge while he took his shower.

I made myself comfortable on one of the easy recliner chairs and flipped through the channels. It was a nice lounge and I had it to myself. I got to watch part of a movie when Clayton came back in. He went downstairs into the store and came back with some soda pop. The telephone beeped that we had a message and Clay smiled. 'We have a preplan', he said. I looked at him and smiled with relief. 'Cool', I said. 'Go check it out and call me if we have to leave right away.' He did and found out we had a load to pick up in Lewiston Idaho by five.

We grabbed meals and snacks for the road and headed west on interstate 90. It was almost 400 miles to Lewiston so I grabbed a quick nap. I would be driving out of there after all and the impending snow storm was on my mind. The clouds were rolling in and while everyone was assuring me that the storm wasn't going to hit until late tomorrow, I was not so sure. I pointed out that I was here and so that meant all bets were off.

We got within an hour of pick up so we called to make sure the load was ready. This customer didn't want you going in unless we had a trailer number and there had been none mentioned in the load assignment. Sure enough, the load wasn't ready yet so we headed straight for the terminal. I wasn't surprised to learn that it was snowing in Butte already. I should have made that bet! We checked with the dispatch window and found out the load still wasn't ready so Clayton went to bed and since I was wide awake with no place to go, I went ahead and got our laundry done. It was a good trade off. It cost only 50 cents to wash there and saved a few dollars since it costs a fortune at the truck stops.

The laundry was finished and I tried to stay awake. I logged onto the internet for a while and couldn't stay awake. It had warmed up outside but it was in the thirties so I knew it was going to snow. Sure enough, there were snowflakes flying around outside, but there wasn't much I could do about it. The dispatcher said he would message the truck as soon as it was ready so I crawled into bed and settled down to sleep. Sure enough, as soon as I got comfortable, the QUALCOM went off. 'I'm not moving', I insisted to my husband. 'He laughed and said he wasn't either. It was snowing out and dark and there was no way we were going anywhere now until morning. It was after 0300 so a few more hours weren't going to hurt. Besides, we were no longer under a time constraint, except for the snow storm that was still going to hit with full force within the next few hours.

Sunday, October 04, 2009

I woke up a few hours later and saw that Clayton was beginning to pull out of the terminal. I got up and asked if he needed help getting to the customer. He said no, of course. We'd been to this customer so many times in the past it was second nature by now. We got our load and headed over to the truck stop to scale the load. Luckily, it wasn't too heavy and we were on our way to Georgia.

I looked out around sleeping Lewiston. I sighed. It was a beautiful area. The drive on 95 south from Lewiston to Boise is a breathtaking view. It follows along the Snake River and is just gorgeous. I missed out on the view this time since it wasn't quite light out yet. And I'd only slept a couple of hours so I went back to bed.

I woke up in time to see Boise. This is one area where I would love to live if I'd been given the chance. It was raining and the temperatures were dropping. I was informed that there had been snow on and off but nothing too bad. For him, I thought. I decided to go back to bed. If I didn't see what was coming, I was happier.

47

We decided not to take interstate 80, which was our route line. The roads were beginning to get slippery and we wanted to get the load to the customer on time, with us in one piece so we opted to go south of Salt Lake City and take hwy 6 east. It was my turn to drive so naturally, by the time I got to the summit of the pass just before Price City, it was snowing there also. I relaxed as I got east of Price City and saw the temperatures beginning to climb. I was happy to see the temperature reach the fifties by the time I got to Green River on Interstate 70.

I pulled into the truck stop there and grabbed a hot dog. I walked Piper and then decided to call it a night. It was almost midnight and though I wasn't really all that tired, I was unsure of the next few hours of driving. Once I got onto the back roads of 198, there were very few places to park. There were a few elevations to climb and I didn't want to risk running into icy roads up there at this time of night. No, it is better to wait for morning. We have until Wednesday to make delivery so there was no pressing need to push on. I grabbed the laptop and began to surf, and write.

Monday, October 5, 2009

We got out of the snow and skirted the storm. I was happy that we had made this decision. This was especially true after calling my Driver Manager to see about getting a reroute done and finding out about drivers stuck up there in Wyoming. He said one of his drivers called and said he was doing about fifteen miles an hour on interstate 80. I had to laugh. Driver Manager yelled for the driver to get off the phone and pay attention to what he was doing.

I had to agree but I can't help but think back to the time we'd hit bad weather on interstate 70 a year ago. A tornado was coming at us and there really wasn't any place to pull over. We headed for the rest area, which turned into a race. Which would get there first? Us, or the tornado? But anyways, I had called the terminal and told them we were headed for the rest area because of the tornado. The dispatcher told me to be sure to send a message via the QUALCOM. I recall thinking 'Yeah Right. I'll get right on that...After the tornado passes.

There are not many safe havens where truckers can go to get away from bad storms. Some of these tornado alleys have two lane roads with no shoulders. I would hope that someday this would change. Many customers won't even allow drivers inside their buildings, even if there is a tornado in their front yard. That happened in Memphis a few years back. It makes you think shake your head.

Clayton and I talked about the previous day and were happy we came out of it alright. He waited until now to tell me about the truck that had jack-knifed on interstate 84, right in front of him. Luckily for that driver, he was able to keep the tractor and trailer upright.

I took over driving in Santa Rosa, New Mexico. After being rerouted, we thought we'd be able to make delivery by late Tuesday night. We'll see. Neither of us took into account the amount of fog on the road so that was sure to slow us down.

I shake my head at how little drivers of smaller vehicles think they are bullet proof. I slowed down to drive through Clyde, Texas and a small white car decided to turn in front of me from the left lane into a convenience store parking lot. What are these people thinking?

I stopped in Quanah, Texas for a short break. They have a really nice rest area with a huge parking lot. I should take pictures and send them to other states to demonstrate what a rest area should look like.

I made it to Fort Worth and shut down for the night...of course, it's 0300 on Tuesday by now. Time for some sleep!

Tuesday, October 6, 2009

I woke up to a large, exploding sound. I heard Clayton mutter a curse and then heard air brakes as the truck came to a stop. Then I heard the door open. It sounded like a tire blow but wasn't sure. It was loud and I'd been asleep. Sure enough, the door opened again and in climbed Clayton. He confirmed it was a flat tire so we headed to the closest terminal, thankful we were near one.

Due to layoffs and cutbacks, the shop is closed at night now. It opens at 0600. Hoping they can fit us in first thing. This load has to get there. It's a hot load, according to the paper work. Ah well, may as well go back to sleep. There is nothing I can do at the moment and Clayton seems to have it under control.

So much for making delivery tonight. We'll make delivery in the morning, but at least we'll still make our delivery time. We just hoped to make it there early. We're deciding whether we want to shut down for a day or keep going. We both have hours so we may wait to shut down, but the temptation to take a day off is strong. We'll see, I suppose.

It is ten o'clock in the evening and I am done for the night. The customer is closed so we will make delivery in the morning.

My shift was uneventful for the most part. I marvel at how, after four years of driving a truck that I still can't seem to get it together when I go into a weigh station. Every other time, I have no real issues when it comes to down shifting. But apparently, when it comes to entering weigh stations, it changes everything. Not just once tonight, but twice, I spent the entire time in the weigh station fighting to down shift. Of course, nobody at the weigh station suspected a thing since I was able to maintain the proper speed. I think the weigh master in Mississippi snickered a little as I kept braking. All in all, I've come a long way in the past four years. I seldom enter the weigh stations. Normally, I get the bi-pass signal or the weigh station is closed.

As with every other night, I kept myself entertained by listening to satellite radio. Tonight, I listened to the Trucking Bozo. I then listened to CNBC and Fox News as well as Headline News. I try to stay away from the political stations lately. I'm kind of an in the middle person politically but I listen to all of the hype on both sides and take a break from it often. It just makes me shake my head at the discontent growing around me. Sometimes, ignorance is bliss.

Wednesday, October 7, 2009

We made delivery on time and without a hitch. We decided to take the rest of the day off. Neither of us is feeling very well today. Clayton is really not feeling well. One of the worst things about driving a truck for a living is when one or both of us gets sick. It can be miserable out on the road.

We opted to get a hotel room. There are no hotels in the Atlanta area that has truck parking. Sure, we can go to the Decatur terminal and drop our empty. We can bobtail to a hotel, but there are few places around that allow pets. None that we would want to stay in anyways.

I found a couple of hotels about thirty miles north of Atlanta that has truck parking. This way, we don't lose our empty trailer and won't waste half a day looking for one tomorrow. I called the Best Western reservation line and found out their hotel on interstate 75, exit 77 has truck parking. They also allow pets. We are heading that way now.

Well, it turns out this hotel does not allow truck parking. It was also very difficult to turn around and get back on the interstate. We turned left at the light and made our way down the road. None of the businesses allowed trucks in their parking lots. We finally managed to get back on the interstate and went to the Super 8 instead. They had ample parking for trucks and allow pets. Very nice staff.

We had lunch at the Mexican restaurant next door to the hotel and ordered Italian for dinner. We will make our way to Walmart tomorrow to restock the truck. I'm not sure if we will leave out with another load tomorrow or take the day off. We shall see in the morning.

Thursday, October 8, 2009

Neither of us was feeling well this morning so we took the day off. One of the disadvantages of being truck drivers is getting sick. It is miserable being in the truck when we're sick. It is also miserable that we get to take time off and spend it laying about in a hotel room when we're in the midst of an exciting city and can't enjoy it.

We did get to Walmart and restocked the truck so we are set when we leave out tomorrow. Hopefully, we'll be feeling better because we need to run the rest of the week. We're taking a vacation in a couple of weeks and really can't afford to take more time off.

Still, it is good to get out of the truck and it is a relief we are able to be sick in a hotel room rather than in a truck stop. It's bad enough that we have to walk across the parking lot to the truck stop, only to walk across the store to get to the bathrooms. It seems like a longer walk when you're sick.

I talked to my sister tonight, like I do just about every night. It is hard to be out here when I have family I can't see whenever I want. That is the other disadvantage of being out on the road. My husband and I don't get to see anybody very often. At best, we take a few days off each month. We do our restarts wherever we happen to be so it is hard to make visits to anyone.

Our parents are elderly and have been concentrating on seeing them when we can. Our adult children see us seldom, though we call them often. We miss seeing our grandchildren. We often talk about moving back to Wisconsin so we are closer to everyone. We have kids and grandkids in Texas, but haven't been able to see them, despite our best efforts. Our schedules just haven't meshed yet and when we get home, they are often working. We usually get home in the middle of the week, mostly in the middle of the night. We take maybe two to three days off and spend the first day catching up on sleep. We spend the second day running around doing errands and maybe visiting whoever is around to visit. The third day, if we have one, is doing fun stuff. I guess we don't have much of a life out on the road.

We occasionally get loads to Wisconsin but either the kids are at work when we're there or we roll through in the middle of the night and can't stop because we are delivering nowhere near them.

Since I'm on a roll about disadvantages on the road, I can also say that it can get lonely. While my husband and I are a team and we spend 24/7 on the truck together, we seldom get to spend any time together. Clayton gets up at three in the morning and drives all day. I start driving around three in the afternoon and usually drive until around two in the morning, sometimes later. We do this daily. We may have a meal together in a truck stop a few times each week, but for the most part; we eat out of the truck. We're on different schedules so it is difficult to do anything together.

We spend time together when we're waiting on a load or if we're doing a restart. We will be spending four days in Orlando at the end of the month with Clayton's brother and sister-in-law. The last time we took that many days off was about two months ago. We spent it at home. We're giving up our apartment at the end of December so will be living out of the truck until spring. This is due mostly because of the economy. It will give us time to perhaps save money to buy a house or condo. If nothing else, it'll give us time to get an emergency fund together if freight slows down again.

We're planning on moving back to Wisconsin, but it changes weekly. We will ultimately end up there but it is so hard to stick to one place at the moment. We see so many beautiful areas of the country that we want to live in all of these places. Of course, after we've gone, we come

52

to our senses. We are at home when we are in Wisconsin. That will, ultimately, be the place we end up (this week anyways as we change our minds daily).

Monday, October 12, 2009

All in all we had a good run. Aside from the fact that both of us were sick and required downtime, we got our load delivered on time. We even had time to stop by the house and check the mail.

Clay was able to get the battery changed in the pickup and then visited with Clint for a while. I stayed home and got caught up on the laundry since the hotel we stayed in did not have laundry facilities. Since Clay also was able to buy a few more storage totes, I was able to pack up most of the kitchen and bathroom.

We are not renewing our lease so the next time we come home, we'll be moving out. It is time to work on paying off the property, or maybe we will move to Wisconsin so we can be closer to some of the kids who really want us to be there.

We have no idea where, exactly we are going but it will be a good move, no matter where we are. The most important thing is we are together.

Chapter 12

Alright, you have read all of the previous chapters and you still want to become a professional driver. Now what? Here are some words to the wise, followed by real-life scenario's to prove my point.

Just because you go to truck driving school does not make you a truck driver. It takes more than a few weeks on the range and it definitely takes longer than a few months to get the hang of things. It will take years to find your comfort zone. It will take even longer before other drivers will consider you a driver.

The trucking community was once called "Knights of the Road". This is because whenever there was a problem on the highways, there was always a truck driver who could offer assistance. As stated in previous chapters, this does not always happen as often, due to a change in the times. People are not as close-knit anymore and sadly, there are criminal minds at work who would like nothing better than to take what isn't theirs.

Here is a case-in-point where the status of "Knights of the Road" can be reinstated in today's society:

Arrow Trucking suspended operations two days before Christmas Eve 2009. The finance companies wanted to repossess the equipment and drivers' fuel cards were turned off. As a result, more than a thousand drivers were stranded hundreds of miles from their homes.

A group of people from the Owner Operator Independent Drivers Association (OOIDA) formed a stranded arrow driver-coordinate efforts here page on Facebook. Within a few hours the page grew to a couple of hundred. Within a week, more than six thousand drivers, former Arrow employees and people not even associated with trucking were helping to locate and assist stranded drivers.

What was just as extraordinary was that other trucking companies jumped in and offered rides to stranded drivers with their own drivers.

Just when the page was beginning to wind down, there came a distress call of a stranded driver whose family had not heard from since before Christmas. The family insisted that this driver would have called home on Christmas Day, had he been able. This information concerned the trucking community and once again, went to work to locate and aid the missing driver. These volunteers contacted radio stations, media outlets, and even America's Most Wanted. As a result, the driver was located.

This is a return to the reinstatement of "Knights of the Road" only it doesn't just apply to truckers, but to every single person who answered the call to help those who couldn't help themselves. It was truly a great thing to see in the midst of economic turmoil. A lot of people gave up their own holidays and savings to ensure these drivers made it home safely for Christmas. It went beyond Christmas Day. These same volunteers were just as hard at work through New Year's Weekend. In fact, the news of the missing driver occurred on January 9, 2010. A great miracle took place. Drivers came together to help their own, and non-drivers gained a new appreciation for the trucking community; One that had never been seen before.

Two very important lessons to learn from the start is this: It is YOUR CDL.

If you get any type of moving violation while operating a commercial vehicle, it is YOUR responsibility to take care of it. The company that employs you may offer to pay the fine; however, they will deduct the expense from your paycheck.

Do not assume your company paid your fine. You do not want to get pulled into a weigh station and find out that your license has been suspended due to nonpayment. Trust me when I say this: The officer at the weigh station could care less whether or not the company paid the fine, especially if he has twenty drivers behind you that he or she needs to inspect. You will be put out of service in a heartbeat and stranded miles away from your home and terminal.

If a company goes out of business and you thought they paid your fine, again, you have no way of backing up your claim. In the end, it is your responsibility to ensure your fine has been paid and keep a record of receipt with you in the event you may need it.

Whether or not your company closes or you pursue a position with another company, your medical card and long form is YOUR responsibility. While companies are required to have a copy of this legally required information, you are also required to have a copy on your person in the event you get stopped and are requested. Again, if you do not have these documents, you will be put out of service. More than likely, you will also get a fine. Also, a potential employer may also ask for these documents when they consider hiring you.

Chapter 13

Do not allow yourself to be a victim. Always be aware of your surroundings and never park anywhere that is not safe. Truck stops and rest areas are great places to park. There are usually a lot of other trucks around and there is safety in numbers.

There is currently legislation introduced to require states to provide safe, adequate parking for truck drivers. This legislation is termed "Jason's Law", after a driver who was robbed and killed in South Carolina. The driver was unable to deliver early so he found parking in an abandoned parking area. It cost him his life. Unfortunately, more drivers are killed in this manner each year and the trucking community is trying to bring awareness of this problem into the public eye.

In the event you are stranded and are miles from home, keep in mind that ultimately, it is you in that position. You may be able to seek assistance from a fellow driver; however, you may not have access to a truck stop or other area where you are likely to come into personal contact.

A cell phone is necessary for conducting business out on the road. You need one in the event you get lost and need directions and you need one so you can keep in touch with your family. It is not a good feeling for your family to not know of your whereabouts and if something happens with your company, your family can help map out your latest route!

Just as important as a cell phone is a cell phone charger. Keep those phones charged! It does you absolutely no good in an emergency if your phone is dead. For emergencies, consider keeping an extra phone on board. This can be a prepaid phone with unused minutes to be used only in the event of an emergency. Again, be sure this phone is fully charged! Bring the charger with you so you can plug it in if you happen to be inside a truck stop. There are outlets which can be used to charge your phone.

Keep a small amount of cash on hand in the event of an emergency and you need to get home. It is also a good idea to have some cash in the event you can't find an ATM machine, or the one you find isn't operational...It's been known to happen.

Each week, take a little cash and buy a prepaid visa gift card. Buy a Walmart gift card, and gift cards for fuel stations. The idea of this is to be prepared in the event that you become stranded, jobless or desperate. These cards can help ease the pain while you are figuring out the next strategy.

If you have a good couple of paychecks and have your bills caught up, go ahead and pay a second or third month in advance. For the same reasons mentioned above, this can help you through the tough times.

Be sure to keep extra food on board. If you had to camp out for a while and you are lucky enough to get home with all of your gear, that extra food can also help you weather the lean times while you look for another job.

Again, keep in touch with your family. Let them know what is going on in your life so they don't worry needlessly. If you have an emergency and do not have a cell phone, ask another driver if you can borrow their phone to call. Remember, most calling plans no longer charge extra for long distance calls. If there is nobody around willing to lend you their phone temporarily, check to see if there is a payphone. You can still call collect!

If there are no other options, ask a manager if you can use the establishment phone. Explain the situation. There is a chance the manager will allow you to use the phone long enough to make a brief call.

For more information and examples, see Appendix B.

Appendix

Trucking Companies who offer Training Schools:

This list is not complete. You must do your due diligence and check out each company before considering them.

Swift Transportation:

http://swift.drivers-central.com/swift-transportation/cdl-training.cfm

Schneider National Inc:

http://www.schneiderjobs.com/

Covenant Transportation:

http://www.covenanttransport.com/

CR England:

http://www.crengland.com/truckdrivingschools/index.jsp

Again, this is a short list of Companies. Do your own research when looking for a driving school.

Articles related to the trucking industry

Truckers for Tots is in full swing

December 8, 9:41 PM, Dallas Trucking Examiner, Rhianna Weir

The holiday shopping season is well underway. The malls around Dallas are packed and everyone seems to be in the holiday spirit.

The truck stops around Dallas are equally as packed as truck drivers stop to fuel their rigs. At the fuel counters are small fliers that are titled 'Truckers for Tots'. Truckers donate a dollar for each form that is filled out. The cashier then hangs up the form with the name of the donor, as well as the company the driver is associated with.

The monies collected are then used to brighten a child's holiday.

If anyone is interested in contributing to this worthy cause, please visit any truck stop and see a cashier. Your contribution will help to provide a great Christmas for a needy child.

A Winter Wonderland blankets the Midwest

December 9, 1:49 PM, Dallas Trucking Examiner,Rhianna Weir

Blizzard conditions kept roads impassible for most of Tuesday night. Wisconsin, Iowa and parts of Illinois were blanketed with snow.

The roads were dangerous enough to keep even the snow plow off the streets.

While blizzards are not very common place here in the Dallas area, it is times like these that make for great opportunities to remind everyone to take extra care during inclement weather. Be sure to keep your fuel tanks full to keep gas lines from freezing and to make sure you do not run out of fuel in the event you become stranded.

Be sure to keep your cell phones fully charged and keep a blanket in your vehicle. It may not get cold often in Dallas but it can and does get cold. It is better to be safe than sorry.

Winter driving tips for Professional Truckers
December 9, 10:48 PM, Dallas Trucking Examiner, Rhianna Weir

A husband and wife team picks up their load in Dallas. They are bound for Green Bay, WI. While it was raining in Dallas when they left, soon they find themselves in colder temperatures. After turning on the weather band, they confirm that there is snow in their forecast.

As the team moves further north they encounter heavy snow. Soon, the highways are moving at a snails pace. The roads are becoming more dangerous and soon they realize they are unable to continue safely.

This scenario is all too familiar and drivers need to take precautions. There is no way to tell how long a highway can be shutdown or how long a storm will cause a delay.

An ample supply of food, water, medicine and clothing is a must. Be sure to have enough essentials to last a few days. Being prepared can keep an already stressful situation from getting worse.

Making Jason's Law a reality
December 10, 1:05 PM, Dallas Trucking Examiner, Rhianna Weir

Jason Rivenburg, from New York, was killed on March 5, 2009, in South Carolina while waiting to deliver his load. He had arrived early and found a safe haven at a deserted gas station. He was robbed and killed, leaving behind a young wife who later gave birth to twins.

Every evening, truck drivers search high and low for a safe place to park their trucks for the night. Some areas are more truck-friendly than others and some outright refuse to allow a driver to park in their vicinity.

Jason's family has taken up the trucker's plight, in the slain driver's memory to have the legislature pass a law that requires all states to provide adequate and safe parking for all truck drivers.

The bill, HR 2156, or Jason's Law was introduced and has since, stalled in the House.

This bill provides a safety net to thousands of drivers who have no legal recourse to protect themselves.

You can support this bill by contacting your state representatives, congressmen and senators. The driver you save could be someone you know.

A heart-warming, snow-melting story
December 12, 1:34 AM, Dallas Trucking Examiner, Rhianna Weir

It was called the first major storm of the year. It was a blizzard. As snow blanketed the Midwest, Truckers looked for shelter. Two drivers, a husband and wife team shut down their rig in a southeastern Wisconsin town called Beloit. The husband drove onto the street that led to the Best Western Hotel and dropped off his wife and dog and most of their baggage at the edge of the driveway. The wife carried the little white dog so as not to make it walk in the snow drifts. I then watched the trucker drive off to park his rig across the street at the truck stop.

I was pleasantly surprised when I saw the front desk clerk of the hotel open the door for the woman. The clerk smiled and petted the dog and helped the woman inside. She checked her in and when she found out the husband had gone to park and was walking back to the hotel she told her not to worry that she would let him know what room she had put them in. I was pleasantly surprised at the reception given to customers here but was in for a few more.

When the husband arrived, he sadly told the woman his daughter lived in town and had been snowed in and so couldn't come meet them. I heard the woman offer this stranger a ride. He was as surprised as I was and at first shyly said no, but this woman insisted that she wasn't going that way and would be no trouble at all. I thought this was beyond customer service at any hotel.

Two days later I watched a bus load of tourists who had lodged for the night leave early that morning after a great breakfast had been served. As these guests left the hotel and boarded their bus, every hotel staff member was at the door waving goodbye.

The hotel was elegant and very well maintained. The staff was super and couldn't complain. I thought I would share this story because we just don't see service like this much anymore. I hope this warms somebody's heart and would carry on the deed.

Holiday travel makes driving a challenge

December 13, 7:23 PM,Dallas Trucking Examiner, Rhianna Weir

The holidays are in the air. People are smiling and waving at one another as they flock to the nearest shopping malls near and far. Establishments are open late and the roads are clogged with passengers with only one goal on their mind.

The only goal that should be on the driver's mind is the traffic in front of them. Unfortunately, this goal is the furthest from many folks minds. With the goal to reach the store and find the closest parking spot, many motorists are putting themselves and everyone around them at risk.

Please take extra care when out and about. With the roads crammed with shoppers and out of town visitors, a trip to your destination can take a detour in a heartbeat. There is no substitute for safe, courteous driving.

Remember that the vehicle that is around you is someone's child, husband, wife, brother or sister. Perhaps, the person you cut off is your own family member.

A wave of cold fronts expected to sweep Dallas area

December 17, 9:29 PM, Dallas Trucking Examiner, Rhianna Weir

A strong cold front is expected to sweep across the area tonight. Two more are expected over the next few days. Now would be a great time to take stock of emergency supplies that are missing from your vehicle.

A blanket, flashlight, and non-perishable food and water are a good recommendation. Check the air pressure on your tires and be sure the fluid levels are filled for both the radiator and windshield washer. Fuel levels should be no less than half-full.

Be careful if you are out and about. Bridges and overpasses could become slippery as well as the road surfaces. Be safe and have a great weekend.

Truck Drivers who park on city streets and alleys risk fines of at least $25 and tow

December 18, 10:37 PM, Dallas Trucking Examiner, Rhianna Weir

Unless you can provide a very good reason for parking on Dallas' city streets, you are subject to a fine of $25. That very good reason had better be mechanical difficulties that prevent the vehicle from being able to be moved by the driver.

The City of Dallas is cracking down on Commercial Vehicles. An anti-idling law is also in effect. Trucks may idle for five minutes every hour.

Dallas is one of several cities in Texas to have such a law. Many states are passing idling laws as a way of curbing emissions problems.

The no idle law is problematic to drivers who are forced to shut down for their federally mandated sleep break. Temperatures inside the cab of a big rig are higher than the outside temperature. Many drivers have pets on board. Pets which are not allowed in most establishments.

There are alternatives to idling which allows a driver to live comfortably inside their truck but those devises range in the thousands of dollars. In our current economic times, enforcement of this law can prove a hardship to America's trucking community.

Have you gotten your H1N1 vaccine yet?

December 19, 8:59 PM,Dallas Trucking Examiner, Rhianna Weir

If you were lucky enough to not get the swine flu yet, you might want to consider getting vaccinated. There is a threat of a second possible wave coming and this is one ride you definitely don't want to ride.

As a Professional Truck Driver, it is very easy to come into contact with many people from all over the country. Getting sick while over the road can be miserable in the best of circumstances. Getting the swine flu several hundred miles away from home is even worse.

If you do begin to show symptoms of the flu while out on the road, here are some tips.

Call your carrier and let them know that you are feeling sick.

If you are able to get into a truck stop, do NOT get out of your truck. Get on the CB radio if you have one and give your truck number and location to a fellow driver. Let them know you are sick and are in need of assistance. Most truck stops are prepared for this situation and will arrange medical attention for you if necessary.

Staying in your truck helps contain the flu and prevents you from spreading it to other drivers.

Stock up on supplies now. Cold Medicines, tissues and blankets are necessary. Be sure to have some canned foods such as soup available. If you have a microwave on board, microwavable soups are available. You can also make hot tea, which will help soothe a sore throat. Ginger tea works well.

If you think you have the swine flu, do not try to ride this out alone. Let someone know of your illness so you can be treated in a timely manner.

Winter weather is certain to make holiday travel hazardous
December 21, 5:18 PM,Dallas Trucking Examiner,Rhianna Weir

Another cold front is expected to make its way across the country; This time from the Northwest.

If you are planning to travel this holiday season, be sure to stay tuned to changing weather conditions and plan accordingly.

Be safe and keep your company abreast of the conditions out there. There is no substitute for safety and the goal is to get freight delivered, not only on time, but in one piece, driver included.

If you are traveling through the Dallas-Fort Worth area and you find yourself in falling temperatures, keep an eye on the overpasses. They tend to freeze before the road surfaces, making travel difficult.

If in doubt, pull over. As always, be sure you have plenty of food and water in your cab. You never know where you will get stuck at and there won't always be a truck stop nearby.

Stranded drivers scramble to get home
December 22, 5:17 PM, Dallas Trucking Examine, rRhianna Weir

Most of the time, trucking companies are scrambling to get their drivers home so they can spend Christmas with their families. By Thanksgiving, drivers are warned to put in for their home-time to ensure an on time arrival.

This week, one trucking company is closing their doors. Did they honor their drivers' requests to get them home for Christmas? No.

Drivers for Arrow Trucking were notified to take their equipment to the nearest Freightliner shop if they have a Freightliner or Kenworth truck. If they have an International Truck, to call back for more information.

Bus tickets are being given out in exchange, but many of these drivers are hundreds of miles away from home. Fuel cards have been turned off by Arrow Trucking. Many of these drivers have pets, microwaves, televisions and more stuff than can possibly fit on a bus.

Arrow Drivers can reach a recorded message at (918) 445-5700.

Arrow Trucking could not be reached for further comment.

In their time of need, strangers jump in to help stranded drivers
December 22, 8:02 PM, Dallas Trucking Examiner, Rhianna Weir

Arrow Trucking closed their doors, stranding at least 1400 drivers all over the country. Drivers were told to bring their trucks to the closest Freightliner shop and, in turn, drivers would be issued bus tickets to get home.

One reader commented that their Son and his wife were one such unlucky driver. "The truck was their home and they had not just what was mentioned in the previous article, but also tools and equipment they were required to purchase."

According to the reader, the bus tickets were not issued by Arrow Trucking, but by a finance company.

Strangers rushed to these drivers' aid. Truckers from other companies, and Owner Operators offered rides and helped get these stranded drivers personal possessions home.

A big thank you is being extended by the reader to everyone who was so kind and generous in these drivers' time of need.

Support coordinated for stranded Arrow drivers
December 23, 1:22 AM, Dallas Trucking Examiner, Rhianna Weir

Support for Stranded Arrow Drivers have coordinated on Facebook. If anyone would like to help, please follow this link...

http://www.facebook.com/pages/Support-for-Stranded-Arrow-Trucking-Drivers-Coordinate-Efforts-HERE/213591833387?ref=search&sid=1070951485.3537977976..1

A great big gratitude of thanks to all who have coordinated these efforts to help these drivers out!

The Trucking Community rallies to the aid of stranded Arrow drivers
December 23, 3:33 AM, Dallas Trucking Examiner, Rhianna Weir

"My husband tells me of an older Arrow driver stuck at the fuel island in Tonapa Az after they allowed him to put 400 dollars of fuel into Arrows truck on Monday morning and Arrow hasn't paid and the TA truck stop exit 103 isn't allowing him to leave, he has no food or money! When my husband was there, a few Arrow drivers helped him through today! Is anyone near there that can help him to get home, fed or whatever need he has? He is in his late 50 early sixties! My husband is not home yet as I said before and asked me to post this Thanks "

This story is one of many coming out of very weary and frustrated Arrow Trucking Drivers, friends, families and other truckers who are witnessing the chaos.

People like Valerie Wright, Beth Stewart, David Wiltrout, Michael Frybarger, Lee Martinez and many many more have offered rides, clothes, showers, a place to sleep and support to these drivers.

As one reader who commented on a previous article, the trucking community is a big, close-knit family and the response from the trucking community proves it.

In spite of Arrow Trucking's behavior, other trucking companies have shown their compassion and have outreached to the stranded drivers as well.

"LinkAmerica has openings and asking Arrow drivers to call 918-828-7620. Kelworth Trucking in Poteau will help with getting drivers home 1-800-331-3399 ext. 216. C Bean Transport in Fort Smith, Ar helping with getting drivers home and has jobs 1-888-646-2177. ABCO Transportation, Spirit Express Trucking, and Paramount Freight Systems has numerous openings in all states-would really like to help any of the drivers that lost their jobs at Arrow 1-866-208-5195. Prime, Inc. wants to help get drivers home and has job openings 800-224-4585. These are just a few of the companies that have stepped up to help the Arrow drivers."

It is a race against time to ensure an on-time delivery of stranded Arrow Drivers
December 24, 10:05 AM, Dallas Trucking Examiner, Rhianna Weir

It is the day before Christmas and the country is being searched high and low for stranded Arrow Drivers.

The entire trucking community has come together at the facebook forum dedicated to seek and aid stranded drivers. A hotline has been set up for a driver to call for assistance. Strangers, both drivers and those not even associated with the trucking industry are lending a helping hand.

"AMAZING!!!! as of now, there are over 3000 people here trying to help these drivers in any way they can, and you can't even open Arrow Trucking's website. REALLY SAD!!!!!"

"The biggest problem is that it might be hard for some of the "oldschool" truckers to see this... Some of them don't carry laptops."

A winter wonderland envelopes Dallas
December 24, 5:54 PM, Dallas Trucking Examiner, Rhianna Weir

Last night felt like a warm spring breeze with rain in the forecast. Today that warm breeze turned cold as a cold front made its way into our area. Rain and snow mix turned to solid snow today, making the roads slick.

In Arlington, the ground is white and the snow continues. As the sun sets the temperatures are expected to drop, making road conditions icy at best.

Be safe and allow extra time to get to your destination. Have a very Merry Christmas!

Stranded Arrow Drivers finding their way in spite of obstacles
December 24, 7:31 PM,Dallas Trucking Examiner,Rhianna Weir

Stranded?

Please call OOIDA at 800-444-5791 for help getting home or share your story if you've made it home.

In a position to help? Please post in the Discussion tab.

Media inquiries: norita_taylor@ooida.com

This is what America's truckers are doing. They didn't wait for anybody to step in. They organized and are seeing results. According to entries on facebook, it is estimated that at least 60% of Arrow Drivers have made their way home. That still leaves 40% unaccounted for.

The obstacle? It is being said on facebook that Arrow Drivers are afraid to pull in anywhere. Apparently, truck stops have been instructed to report any Arrow truck to the Company so these trucks can be repossessed. Drivers are getting two stories. Some are being told they can bobtail home and turn in trucks closer to home, while others are having their keys taken away from them, stranding them right where they stop.

Still, this isn't stopping truckers from stepping up and offering rides to weary stranded drivers. Companies and individual Owner Operators, alike, are pulling together all efforts to ensure a safe return home.

Attention all 4-Wheelers!
December 25, 12:07 AM,Dallas Trucking Examiner,Rhianna Weir

I was just talking to a driver who is traveling on interstate 20 westbound in Grand Prairie. The roads are very icy and said that cars are cutting in front of him as he tries to maintain a safe distance.

Please be aware that these trucks cannot stop fast enough on dry roads and cutting these truckers off creates a very hazardous situation.

Please, if you see a truck, give them wide berth and allow them to maintain that spacing. If an accident or other incident occurs in front of them and you get between it, there is no way to stop.

Please be cautious and leave yourself a way out. Be safe and let's all have a safe and Merry Christmas.

The true meaning of Christmas shines bright for the trucking community

December 25, 10:32 AM,Dallas Trucking Examine,rRhianna Weir

It is Christmas Day and people are nestled all snug in their homes, surrounded by family and celebrating the day, right? Not quite.

While most families are actually celebrating Christmas with their families, there are many Arrow Truckers who have yet to make it home. There are thousands of truckers out there who have put their festivities on hold in order to help bring their fellow drivers home.

To date, the amount of support has risen to over 4000 volunteers who have joined this crusade, and it isn't just truck drivers. People who have no affiliation with the trucking industry are rushing to the aid of stranded drivers, opening their homes and wallets.

If they can't get them home, they are looking for jobs for these drivers and getting them into another truck, which is home to many of these drivers.

Some trucking companies have hotlines set up to assist these drivers with finding jobs, transportation and assistance.

Arrow Drivers are being found around the country. A driver will then put a message on a page on facebook dedicated to helping stranded drivers. Within seconds, efforts are coordinated to get assistance to that driver.

Facebook is not the only venue where these coordination efforts are taking place. Isaac Eiland-Hall has set up a site that features coordinated efforts, by state.

It is indeed, the true meaning of Christmas!

Record Winter Storm in Texas creates icy conditions

December 25, 11:23 AM,Dallas Trucking Examiner,Rhianna Weir

Yesterday's snow storm broke records. It also broke wallets as the storm caused multiple accidents and road closures throughout North Texas.

On US 287, many professional drivers are making a snails pace attempt to get their loads delivered in a safe and timely manner. 'There are multiple trucks and cars all over the place in ditches and snowbanks', said one driver.

The 635 loop around Dallas was shut down last night. Interstate 20 was closed around the Weatherford area. Many roads were closed from North Dallas into Oklahoma.

Around the Country, many roads were closed due to winter weather conditions, but this is Dallas. It is rare to see such accumulations in this part of the country.

The giving continues beyond stranded drivers

December 25, 12:35 PM,Dallas Trucking Examiner,Rhianna Weir

'I am seeing flat bed truckers pulling big rigs out of ditches on us-287 just south of Wichita Falls, Texas.'

The response of the trucking industry to the needs of stranded Arrow Drivers has been tremendous. Now we are seeing the same caring response from drivers who are traveling north from Fort Worth, Texas on the US 287 highway, where ice and snow continues to make travel difficult.

A truck has hijacked on the bridge in Wichita Falls, creating a long delay. The road has just reopened and traffic is slowly moving.

According to the Texas DOT, once the drivers push north of Mount Vernon, the roads are clear.

It is now a hide and go seek game for stranded Arrow Drivers
December 25, 9:06 PM, Dallas Trucking Examiner, Rhianna Weir

They were told to turn in their trucks to a nearby Freightliner shop. They were told they would be given bus tickets home in exchange for turning in the trucks. Drivers who had equipment other than a Freightliner or Kenworth truck were told to sit tight for more information on where to turn those trucks in.

When some Arrow Drivers turned in their equipment, they found out their non-driving spouses were not eligible for bus tickets. Neither were pets. Up to four bags per passenger were permitted.

Fuel cards were turned off, leaving many drivers stranded at truck stops with no way of getting their trucks anywhere.

Arrow Trucking did nothing to help these stranded drivers. It took other drivers and other companies to come together to assist these strangers. Food, fuel, rides, a warm place to sleep and much more were offered.

Tonight, there are reports of people pretending to be Arrow Drivers in order to take advantage of the generosity of the trucking community. There are people pretending to be repo agents and trying to steal trucks and cargo. There are reports of weigh stations and DOT officers looking for Arrow drivers, not to help, but make things worse by taking the drivers keys when the driver is trying to get home. Even though many of these drivers had made arrangements to turn in their trucks after they get home. Many of these drivers live in their trucks and have no place to go.

In spite of all of the obstacles, there are thousands lined up and waiting to assist the stranded drivers.

Information for Arrow Drivers

December 26, 10:35 AM,Dallas Trucking Examine,rRhianna Weir

A comment was made upon reading previous articles about the stranded Arrow Drivers. Navistar Financial Corporation is trying to contact drivers who have International trucks.

"Navistar Financial Corporation - Attention Arrow drivers: If you are driving an International, please take it to the nearest International dealership. Navistar Financial wants to help you get home and is offering a bus ticket or $200 cash. For help, please call Navistar Financial at 800-233-9121 and select #3 for customer service. If you call outside of business hours, please leave a message with your name, a phone number where we can reach you, your current location, and the VIN number of your truck."

The contact number listed above does go to Navistar Financial and office hours are Monday-Friday.

Arrow Trucking closed its doors on Tuesday, leaving more than 1400 drivers to find their own way. Finance Companies, trying to recover their equipment are offering bus tickets or a reimbursement of up to $200 when drivers turn in their equipment.

Help continues to pour in for the stranded Arrow drivers

December 26, 5:15 PM,Dallas Trucking Examiner,Rhianna Weir

He no longer has a job, a car or a home. He is living at a hotel that was paid for when he turned in his Arrow truck.

Drivers are still stranded and others made it home but are at a loss of what to do. "We haven't had a paycheck in a month and we have bills that can't be paid."

Arrow Trucking closed its doors, leaving drivers stranded all over the country and office personnel scrambling to figure out their next move.

76

"Where is the national attention?" A lot of unanswered questions pile in and thousands of people, some not affiliated with the trucking industry, are doing their best to ease the concerns and fears of these people whose lives have been turned upside down.

The weather doesn't stop the generosity for stranded drivers
December 27, 4:36 AM, Dallas Trucking Examiner, Rhianna Weir

All across the country, there is a massive push to scour every inch, in search of what is left of the stranded Arrow driver. While most of these drivers have made it home, several are still out there. Many of the drivers who remain stranded have no home to go to. These drivers lived in their trucks.

"We have one driver in Vegas living out of his pickup." While many drivers have families to support, others do not and lived in their trucks because they spent little time at 'home'. There seemed no reason to pay for an apartment they rarely lived in.

The outpouring of support to help these drivers in need has been phenomenal. "It brings tears to my eyes that so many cared about my husband getting home", said the wife of an Arrow driver.

With the major snowstorm causing road closures throughout the country, it did not stop the effort to bring the drivers home.

Truck Drivers and non-truck drivers, alike, drove out in the weather, without a care for their own comfort, to aid another. "It truly shows that the true American spirit is still alive and well".

More snow on the way
December 27, 10:17 PM,Dallas Trucking Examiner,Rhianna Weir

Christmas Eve 2009 saw a record snow accumulation for the Dallas area. More is on the way. Cold weather has arrived and it's here to stay.

More snow is expected for Tuesday, although it is not expected to be a record-breaker this time around. Still, the area expects icy conditions and now is the time to prepare.

As always, leave enough time to get to your destination. Be sure to have extra supplies on your truck, in the event of road closures, which will certainly delay your travel.

Be safe and remember, the best place to be in icy conditions is parked.

The Women in Trucking Association continues to help women break barriers
December 28, 10:30 AM,Dallas Trucking Examiner,Rhianna Weir

Ellen Voie, author of 'Crushing Cones' set up Women in Trucking Association as a way "to encourage the employment of women in the trucking industry, promote their accomplishments and minimize obstacles faced by women working in the trucking industry."

Women can go to Women in Trucking Association's website and see the various links meant to give information from companies hiring to support.

You can meet Ellen at the Mid-West Trucking show in Peoria, Illinois-Booth 105. She will also be at the Mid-America Trucking show in Louisville, Kentucky.

Where are the lawmakers when you need them?
December 28, 11:35 AM, Dallas Trucking Examiner, Rhianna Weir

The trucking industry is a highly regulated entity. Every inch of this industry has to have its T's crossed and I's dotted. Hours of Service Regulations are in place to ensure safety for both the driver and the public.

Weigh Stations are in place to ensure the freight a driver is hauling is both safely secured and within the parameters of each states restrictions.

Log Books are a fact of life for every driver out there. A driver even has to document when they shut down to eat or use facilities, or for anything that takes more than seven minutes.

Trucking companies are going down by the head in recent months and there is no safety net for its drivers.

Arrow Trucking is just another example of the state of affairs of the economy; however, in this case, Arrow provided absolutely no warning or assistance to its employees, leaving the rest of the trucking industry to clean up its mess.

There should be safeguards set up that ensures the rights of our nations professional drivers. Arrow suspended operations but because they did not lay off their workers, nobody was able to file for unemployment.

This is the norm across all of the trucking industry. It is a rare feat for a professional driver to be able to collect unemployment because basically, nobody really fires or lays off anyone.

Also, if a driver is leased on with a company, they are considered to be self-employed. In the event of a layoff or if a company goes under, leaving drivers stranded, these 'self-employed' lease operators are normally not eligible for relief.

Where is the support for these drivers and why are these companies able to get away with this practice?

There needs to be a change in the way Professional Drivers are treated.

Call your lawmakers and demand the rights that are given to every other workplace member.

Questions still unanswered for over a thousand Arrow Trucking employees

December 28, 7:58 PM, Dallas Trucking Examiner, Rhianna Weir

"What now?" asks many Arrow employees, drivers and office staff, alike. "We are jobless but are considered employed because Arrow suspended operations. There is no layoff so we can't file for unemployment."

"I spent money out of my own pocket for fuel to get home. I turned the truck in but I still have bills to pay."

"I lived out of my truck and am now homeless."

These are just a few of the unanswered questions being asked by the employees at Arrow Trucking. There has yet to be a response from the owners of the trucking company. There were rumors that the company filed for bankruptcy but so far that has not been confirmed.

Arrow Trucking closed their doors last Tuesday and left all of its drivers, scattered all over the country and hundreds of miles from home, to fend for themselves.

Volunteers from all walks of life stepped up to help. Other trucking companies stepped in to offer assistance. Recruiters from trucking companies are vamping up the effort to recruit those left to pick up the pieces.

The Owner Operators Independent Drivers Association started the Facebook page to assist these drivers.

"Arrow drivers, please refer to the links section if you are looking for jobs. OOIDA has compiled a list of some companies offering jobs. Recruiters, you can forward your offers via e-mail to angel_burnell@ooida.com."

"Still have your truck? Need your last paycheck? You have questions, OOIDA is getting the answers. Check it out on the Links tab. Look for the FAQ link."

For those based out of Tulsa, Workforce Oklahoma has stepped up to help.

"Remember Workforce Oklahoma will be holding a special "Rapid Response" event for those put out of work by Arrow Trucking. Covers everything from filing for unemployment to applying for jobs. Workforce says they've already heard from upwards of 20 companies looking to hire."

It is hoped that the stranded drivers and displaced office workers will have the answers they seek soon.

Stranded and homeless in Dallas and Fort Worth area
December 29, 5:44 PM, Dallas Trucking Examiner, Rhianna Weir

All across the country are the many Arrow drivers who were left to fend for themselves after Arrow Trucking closed its doors. More than a thousand drivers were told through satellite qualcom units that operations were suspended and for drivers to turn in their trucks and trailers, some with loads, to the nearest Freightliner or Daimler dealer. It took a few days but those with International trucks to be given instructions.

One week later, some drivers are still trying to get home and although a massive effort is underway to locate and assist these drivers, there is more need.

Some of these drivers are homeless. Some of these drivers need assistance with utilities, rent and the basic essentials. This need is due to the fact that nobody in this company has had a paycheck in at least a month.

Some charities, such as trucker charity are available but funds are needed.

Weir It Solutions is accepting donations in exchange for a book.

For more information see links below.

There are many drivers in need right here in Dallas. Drivers are stranded and are in need of a place to stay and a warm meal while they figure out their next step.

If anyone would like to help please see the below link

http://www.facebook.com/#/SupportArrowTruckers?ref=nf

http://sites.google.com/site/weiritsolutions/home?previewAsViewer=1

http://www.truckercharity.org/

The crisis that gathered thousands of professional drivers together
December 30, 10:28 PM, Dallas Trucking Examiner, Rhianna Weir

A week ago, drivers had only a few things on their minds. They had to pick up and deliver their freight, and they had to get home to celebrate Christmas with their loved ones.

Last Tuesday changed all that. Thousands of 'Knights of the Highway' put aside their own agendas to concentrate on a new one...Get the stranded Arrow drivers home.

The quest to find and assist drivers have remained the goal as we head into New Years Eve. While many prepare to share in the festivities of the new year, many remain vigilant. Their goal to find, assist and bring home the remaining drivers.

It is truly a wonderful thing to see as the year draws to a close. May the New Year of 2010 continue these great deeds.

Professional Drivers now have access to medical care on the road

December 31, 6:41 AM,Dallas Trucking Examiner,Rhianna Weir

They leave home for a three week stretch. They pick up their first load and deliver it efficiently and safely. While waiting on their next load, a husband and wife team gets sick. What do they do? They are two hundred miles away from home and are too sick to move their truck safely.

The family doctor understands the fact that his patients can't get to the office but does not want to diagnose and treat an illness blindly. Therefore, these drivers can't get the personal medical attention they need and deserve. They don't know what to do. Their truck and trailer is too large to fit in a local doctor's parking lot.

This story is true for just about every professional truck driver on the road. Fortunately, one doctor has recognized this problem and has come up with a solution.

Doctor John Mc Elligot has been working with drivers for several years. He spearheaded clinics at truckstops and served the trucking community well until financial difficulties forced them to close.

Recently, Doctor Mc Elligot announced a call center that caters to drivers medical needs. This is a subscription-based service that allows a driver access to a doctor 24 hours a day, seven days a week.

The call center costs $29.95 per month for a driver, and $39.95 monthly for an entire family to join. Members of the call center obtain discounts through a prescription benefit program.

For more information and to sign up for this valuable resource, call 877-514-TRUC (8782) for service.

New Years Eve celebrations don't always mix with driving

December 31, 2:15 PM,Dallas Trucking Examiner,Rhianna Weir

Tonight's Festivities are sure to be a celebration to remember. After all, it is the end of a decade and there is so much to celebrate. There is also much to despair.

Many out there are celebrating, paying no attention to the amount of alcohol they are consuming, let alone how they are getting home safely.

If you find yourself out on the road tonight, take extra care as you are maneuvering yourself through towns and cities. This is especially important between the hours of 10pm-6am. If you can, pull over between these hours to avoid a potentially dangerous situation that can and does often occur.

If you are enjoying the festivities and are planning to drink alcoholic beverages, keep in mind that AAA has offered free rides. Make a plan for a designated driver.

The police presence in Dallas will be extra vigilant tonight. They are looking for drunk drivers, speeders and those not wearing seat-belts.

Happy New Year and please be safe!

A highlight of what happened in the transportation industry in 2009

January 1, 12:45 PM,Dallas Trucking Examiner, Rhianna Weir

It is a new year, a new decade. Out with the old, in with the new. What were the events that stood out for 2009?

The most recent highlights the problems that plague the industry. Arrow Trucking closed its doors, leaving its employees stranded, jobless and demanding answers and justice.

Arrow Trucking is the latest in a long line of failures that is plaguing the trucking industry. The past two years has seen an epidemic of companies, both small and large either going under completely or seeking bankruptcy protection in an attempt to reorganize.

A few states, such as Minnesota and Indiana developed the infamous Driver Fatigue checklist, resulting in many drivers being put out of service or fined. There is a suit pending against this practice.

The 'Convoy for a Cure' event took place in an effort to raise awareness and funds for Breast Cancer

There is the ongoing debate about the Mexican Truck Pilot Program that allows Mexican drivers to conduct business in the United States. Whether or not this program is valid, safe or economically sound to our country remains a heated debate.

Many roadside clinics that were available to truck drivers were closed due to financial reasons. This problem of not having the medical care while on the road prompted the opening of a 24-hour call center to address these needs.

Changes to the hour of service regulations are on going and perhaps will be resolved in 2010, along with a multitude of other transportation issues.

These are just a few of a myriad of issues regarding the transportation industry in 2009.

Drivers still unaccounted for
January 2, 3:11 PM, Dallas Trucking Examiner, Rhianna Weir

There has been an ongoing attempt on the behalf of countless volunteers to account for the whereabouts of the hundreds of Arrow drivers that were left stranded last week.

While many have made it home, both on their own accord and through countless efforts through generous donations on the part of other drivers as well as trucking companies, many are still out there.

It is estimated that more than four hundred drivers are unaccounted for. This may be due to the inability of a driver to contact anyone. They might not have access to the internet, nor funds to call.

Many drivers were living in their trucks. These drivers may not have resources to get anywhere.

There is a movement to try to locate and assist these missing drivers.

Where are all of the loads?
January 2, 4:36 PM, Dallas Trucking Examiner, Rhianna Weir

While there has been a tremendous effort to get stranded Arrow Trucking drivers home, there has been little light put on another potentially dangerous situation.

Where are all of the hundreds of loads that never made it to their customers?

The Federal Motor Carrier Safety Administration (FMCSA) is asking the same question.

When Arrow Trucking suspended operations, fuel cards were shut off by their suppliers, leaving many drivers unable to move their loads. Arrow Trucking was directed by the FMCSA to account for, and move these loads to a secure location.

The question remains as to the whereabouts of these loads.

If anyone has any information regarding these loads, or wants to make a complaint, please call:

1-888-DOT-SAFT (368-7238)

A new light shines on America's trucking community
January 3, 9:31 AM, Dallas Trucking Examiner, Rhianna Weir

Out of the mess that began with Arrow Trucking suspending operations just two days before Christmas Eve, a new dawn of enlightenment has surfaced from the trucking community across this country.

The professional drivers can hold their heads up and once again be called true Knights of the Road. They have earned this right through the benevolence and generosity they have shown to their own.

These knights did not know the drivers in need but they sought out an Arrow driver, offered comfort in the way of food, lodging and fuel. They bought bus tickets, plane tickets and put drivers up in hotels. They bought pizza and gift cards. They transferred funds through credit cards, comdata cards and paypal.

Drivers relayed the stranded across the country through cooperation of other drivers in an effort to get them home safely.

Some drivers put the stranded on buses and relayed their belongings close to their home so they would not lose their possessions.

Complete strangers, drivers and non-drivers alike, opened their homes to the stranded. They offered them showers, meals and a warm bed until jobs and living arrangements could be found.

Volunteers worked effortlessly, around the clock from December 22, 2009 and continue today.

OOIDA, or the Owner Operators Independent Drivers Association stepped up to the plate from day one. They organized the facebook page, 'Support for Stranded Arrow Drivers-Coordinate Efforts Here'. It was monitored 24 hours/7 days a week. This was where miracles were born. This was where thousands of people congregated with one purpose in mind: To get the Arrow drivers home.

"Thanks to OOIDA and Land Line Now for all their efforts. I wish I could have done something but being home for the holidays, I wasn't out there to give rides or donations to indiviuals, all I could do is pray they all made it home for the holidays safe. A GREAT effort for the organization." Kenny Peterson

The work is far from over. There are still over four hundred drivers unaccounted for and there are still thousands of volunteers vowing to not quit and leave no one behind.

The angels behind the effort
January 3, 1:18 PM, Dallas Trucking Examiner, Rhianna Weir

'Arrow Trucking Volunteer Efforts' consists of volunteers, who evolved from OOIDA's 'Stranded Arrow Drivers Coordinate Here' Facebook page.

Dana Stanley, Eric Mende, Sheri Sauter, and countless others has been at the forefront from the very beginning, coordinating efforts to point other volunteers in the path of a stranded driver in need of assistance.

Their page on Facebook is organized by state and reports who is home and who is in need of assistance. This allows volunteers to tackle an issue on a case by case basis.

The group helps to verify an Arrow driver's identity and does their best to prevent scams from occurring.

They also assist with a job opportunity section, that allows drivers access to a number of company's who are hiring and contact information.

A job well-done is in order for this great effort.

Missing Driver Alert! Have you seen John Eischens?

January 3, 3:20 PM, Dallas Trucking Examiner, Rhianna Weir

John Eischens was a driver with Arrow Transport until they suspended operations. During a phone campaign that is ongoing to account for stranded drivers, it has come to the attention to volunteers for 'Arrow Trucking Volunteers'.

John's family is very concerned. They have not heard from him since before Christmas. His truck number is 6325.

If anyone knows John Eischen or see's an Arrow truck with this truck number, please contact his family and notify the volunteers at the link below:

http://www.facebook.com/#/pages/Arrow-Trucking-Volunteer-Efforts/228810897407?v=wall&ref=nf

Old Man Winter returns with a vengeance

January 3, 10:45 PM,Dallas Trucking Examiner, Rhianna Weir

As the new year begins the first of the work week, something is already at work. Temperatures are expected to drop into the low 30's tonight in the Dallas area and are expected to remain low throughout the day tomorrow.

Old Man Winter is back and he's here to stay. By the end of the week, temperatures along with a dangerous wind chill are expected to be below zero. These temperatures can cause a dangerous scenario.

While there is no precipitation expected, there is a danger of frost bite for long term exposure.

Protect yourself and be sure to bundle up. Be sure your fuel tanks are full and that you have provisions inside the cab of your truck. Spend as little time as you can out of doors.

Exposure to these frigid temperatures can be life threatening. Take care!

Arrow driver is still missing
January 4, 11:24 AM, Dallas Trucking Examiner, Rhianna Weir

John Eischens said goodbye to his mother with a heavy heart. This was a week before Christmas and his family has not heard from him since. He was last known to be hauling a load for Arrow Transport last week but the trucking company suspended operations.

"It isn't like JR not to call for Christmas", says both his mother and sister. The family is worried sick and filed a missing persons report with their local police department.

The efforts of the volunteers at 'Arrow Trucking Volunteer Efforts' have turned up no new leads. The group has coordinated efforts with OOIDA's 'Support for Stranded Arrow Trucking-Coordinate Efforts Here' to find the missing driver.

"We try to call Arrow but all we get is the same recorded message", says one administrator for the site.

Qualcom has been notified and that company tried to get information about the trucks location but were unable to because either the Qualcom unit in the driver's truck is faulty, or he does not have a unit in his truck.

Daimler has been contacted and asked to cooperate by checking to see if Eischens' truck had been turned in or recovered. No new information has been available.

There is no last known location. What is known was that he was under a load but only Arrow Trucking has the critical information of where the load was picked up and where the load was to be delivered. Until that information is gotten, there is no known route line.

This driver is indeed, a needle in a haystack.

Helpful tips to help drivers from getting stranded

January 4, 5:08 PM, Dallas Trucking Examiner, Rhianna Weir

Hindsight is twenty-twenty and it seems that everyone has an opinion as to how drivers could have avoided getting stranded two days before Christmas.

While it is great to offer such opinions, unless someone has been put in such a position, there really is no room for second-guessing. That aside, here are some tips to help ease the burden, should a driver ever find themselves in a similar situation again.

Is there a storage unit near your terminal? If there is, consider renting such a facility to put your belongings in should a need arise. You may want to rent ahead of time so you already have a place to go to. In many instances, a bobtail would fit. If there is anything inside your truck that you aren't using, store them here as well.

An emergency fund is vital. If you don't have an emergency fund in place, start one today. Plan to put a certain amount into this fund and stick to it. You should also keep a certain amount of cash on board in the event that you are nowhere near an ATM machine or are not near a business establishment. Put your loose change in a jar. You can accumulate a substantial savings with that change!

Keep blank comdata or other fleet checks on hand at all times. You never know when you will need them!

Most comdata cards work in an ATM machine! It works like a checking account and Walmart accepts comdata cards at the register.

Be prepared for the unexpected. Have supplies in the truck in case you need to pack in a hurry. Keep emergency contact numbers and be sure to have at least one calling card or visa gift card in the event you may need to call someone. Cell Phones only work if they are charged. Keep those phones charged! If you have a prepaid service, keep extra minutes at all times.

Be aware of your surroundings. Keep phone numbers of other trucking companies. They can be of assistance should you find yourself stranded by your company. Truck stops are full of advertisements with these companies and they even have toll-free numbers.

The welcome centers are filled with lodging information.

Above all, use common sense. If something doesn't feel right, then it probably isn't.

Despite an economic downturn, companies still hiring
January 5, 6:11 AM, Dallas Trucking Examiner, Rhianna Weir

While many companies were downsizing their operations and tightening their belts, many were opening their hearts and doors for Arrow drivers.

During what is considered to be the slowest time of year, many trucking companies reached out to the more than one thousand drivers who were stranded and jobless due to the suspension of operations at Arrow Trucking.

Freight is down but these companies, large and small, opened their hearts to so many who were down. They reached out across the internet and coordinated with both OOIDA and with the city of Tulsa where more than twenty trucking companies participated in a job fair for Arrow employees.

Link America, WSE Transportation, Jim Palmer, Roehl Transportation, C Bean Transport, Knight Transportation, Hoffmeier Incorporated, John Veriha Trucking, Swift Transportation and many many more all stepped up.

Drivers for Schneider, Werner Enterprises, Swift Transportation and countless others sent messages to their employees through the Qualcomm to be on the lookout for any stranded Arrow driver and to offer assistance and rides.

"Richard Stockton, the CEO of Swift Transportation, directed us to offer rides and to contact our driver managers if they were going somewhere different then we were going, to coordinate another option."

In these trying times, it is good to know that companies and good-hearted people can come together to help.

Will the real Arrow Driver please stand up!

January 5, 8:12 AM, Dallas Trucking Examiner, Rhianna Weir

Good-hearted, well-meaning people have opened their time, homes and wallets to aid the stranded Arrow drivers since first discovering that Arrow Trucking suspended operations. These Good Samaritans deserve recognition for their contributions.

While many cases of drivers have sought help through the kindness and generosity of these people, there are those who are seeking to undermine their efforts through scams.

These scam artists are contacting OOIDA and other facebook pages where ongoing efforts to organize and help people with stories of being stranded Arrow drivers.

"A driver claims he is stranded in Canada with no documents to get him across the border'

A person claiming to be a stranded Arrow driver in Missouri needing to get to Georgia was the latest scam that succeeded because while the scam was caught, it was not before money and a bus ticket was given.

"Drivers need to take extra caution when approached. Taking someone into the cab of your truck can be a dangerous proposition if it turns out to be someone claiming to be an Arrow driver and isn't."

Scamming for money is a crime. If anyone has fallen victim to these attempts, report it to your local law enforcement agency.

Missing Arrow driver still unaccounted for

January 6, 3:59 AM,Dallas Trucking Examiner,Rhianna Weir

John Eischens' truck has been found today in Butte, Montana. His truck was stripped clean and there was no sign of his personal possessions.

Hundred of drivers had been searching every truck stop, rest area and truck-friendly venue for three days, since discovering that Eischens' family had not received any word from him.

"It is unheard of that he would not have called on Christmas Day", said John's mother.

While the truck has been found, there is still no sign of this driver. His family is very concerned. He had not received payment from Arrow Trucking in weeks and only worked for the company for about a month.

Upon calling local establishments in the area, no trace of Eischens has been discovered.

It is possible that he may have gotten a ride with another trucker but so far, that has not been confirmed. If anyone has any knowledge of the whereabouts of John Eischens, please go to the link below and let the volunteers at Arrow Trucking Volunteer Efforts know.

Very cold conditions expected

January 6, 12:22 PM, Dallas Trucking Examiner, Rhianna Weir

As the arctic air continues on its southward track, we can all be thankful here that we are not in Fulton, NY where it has snowed for the past nine days. More than four feet of snow has fallen on this town, and it is *still* snowing.

While the Dallas area is not expected to have any precipitation, it is expected to get even colder as Thursday approaches. Temperatures have already dropped below freezing at night here and is expected to drop into the teens tomorrow night. With wind-chills, temperatures are expected to be below zero.

As in other parts of the south, these freezing temperatures can affect any crops in Texas.

The threat to human life is a very real scenario. Frost bite can set in after only a short exposure. Take extra care in preventing exposure to skin. Stay indoors if you can and if you are out of doors, bundle up!

Drivers should take care to have their fuel levels no less than half-full. In the event that you have to get out of your truck, take precautions. Have plenty of food and water in your cab so that you can limit your excursions outside of your truck.

Stranded and jobless Arrow Drivers struggling to make ends meet

January 7, 3:54 AM, Dallas Trucking Examiner, Rhianna Weir

Not only were Arrow drivers surprised to find out they were jobless and stranded across the country, they were also surprised to discover that their paychecks had bounced.

It was like one bad scenario after another. Drivers who made it home safely whether on their own accord or through the assistance of the many 'Knights of the Road', discovered that because of their paychecks bounced, so also did their bills.

"We have had many drivers ask how they were going to pay their bills now. Some had had their phones and electric turned off, while others were facing immediate eviction due to non-payment of their rent." says Facebooks 'Arrow Drivers Volunteer Efforts'.

Many of the stranded now have new jobs with other trucking companies but many have not been as successful. There are still drivers unaccounted for and one driver has been officially missing.

John Eischens' family is concerned and filed a missing persons report. John has been missing for several weeks now and the family has not heard from him. "It is not like John to not call home on Christmas Day."

So what can drivers do to get help?

Call each creditor and explain the situation to them. If the creditor is unwilling to work with you, see what assistance you can get within your community.

Call the mayor's office, your Congressman and your Senator.

Call the American Red Cross, The Salvation Army. If there is a Community Action office, call them.

Your local Church may be able to help provide assistance.

If you have credit card debt, did you also purchase insurance? If so, call them an activate that insurance. In most policies, your account can be frozen for up to six months while you look for a job and get back on your feet.

Most credit card companies will work with you if you keep them updated on what is going on in your life. Some may even waive late payment fees. It never hurts to ask for help.

Where is the National Media in the case of a missing Arrow driver?
January 8, 4:57 PM, Dallas Trucking Examiner, Rhianna Weir

Volunteers and drivers alike are voicing their concerns and frustration at the lack of media attention on missing Arrow Transport driver, John Eischens. In fact, they are frustrated over the lack of media on the entire Arrow fiasco.

Other than a few minutes here and there from local media channels, there have been no real coverage of the over one thousand drivers, office and shop staff that were left stranded and jobless, two days before Christmas.

Volunteers from OOIDA's 'Support for Stranded Arrow Trucking Drivers-Coordinate Efforts Here' has been manned from day one. They have helped get drivers home and have helped coordinate efforts with

'Arrow Trucking Volunteer Efforts' to arrange for help to all Arrow drivers.

'We have contacted the media. We have contacted 'America's Most Wanted'. We have contacted The Nancy Grace Show'.

Many have written to, or called their state legislatures, Senators, Congressmen. Many have even written to President Obama.

"Who are we supposed to call to bring attention to this matter?" says Volunteers.

"We are not third class citizens. We keep America moving by bringing goods into your stores and therefore your homes. We will not give up looking for John Eischens, and we will not rest until every stranded driver is found and accounted for."

Arrow Trucking files for Bankruptcy amidst the desperate search for John Eischens

January 9, 1:21 AM,Dallas Trucking Examiner,Rhianna Weir

Arrow Trucking has several problems. They suspended operations without so much as a warning, leaving its employees jobless and more than a thousand drivers stranded hundreds of miles from their homes.

Today, a new lawsuit was filed against the large carrier by a Utah-based lender, Transportation Alliance Bank, Inc. Arrow faces fraud and racketeering charges.

A class action suit, filed by former Arrow employees, seeks to recover several weeks worth of back-pay from bounced paychecks.

Arrow Trucking, as an employer is responsible for its staff and employees. Their serious lack of judgment has caused hardship across the board. Their actions lead to many drivers who are still unaccounted for. One such driver, John Eischens is missing. There is a nationwide search on the part of thousands of truck drivers and volunteers, who are looking for the missing driver.

The Anna, Texas Police Department and Law Enforcement in Montana have combined efforts to find John as well.

Are anti-idling laws fair?

January 9, 3:47 PM,Dallas Trucking Examiner,Rhianna Weir

Many states, such as California and New York have strict anti-idling laws in effect for commercial vehicles. While not all of Texas has such ordinances, there are a few municipalities in Texas who do. Austin, Arlington and Dallas come to mind.

While these ordinances are seemingly well-justified in the eyes of some, it does not seem to be fair in the eyes of many. Most of these laws are in effect in an effort to cut down on pollution. 'To Go Green", and to be Green is a very popular position these days.

Some companies, such as Walmart and J C Penney's have anti-idling policies in effect. If a driver comes into a facility to pick up a load or make a delivery, they are required to turn off their engines.

It seems like a common procedure these days, but how fair are these practices?

A large majority of drivers spend at least 70 hours a week their cabs. Drivers are required by federal law to spend at least 8 hours in the sleeper with an addition 2 hours either inside the sleeper or inside a truck stop or where ever they happen to be. That is free time. Many drivers live inside their trucks and so spend hardly any time outside it.

Many of the working public spend almost an equal amount of time in their homes. They run air conditioners, heaters, and many electronic equipment without a care in the world, except maybe their electric bills, which can be comparable to fuel costs to run a commercial vehicle.

Many in the general public spend time sitting in drive-thru lanes at establishments such as fast food, banks, car washes...you get the picture. If a driver of a car were sitting in traffic, they would also idle their vehicles.

The point is, according to many drivers, is that if a car owner or suv owner was required to spend more time in their vehicles, they would also idle their vehicles to be comfortable. This would be especially true in the hot summer months and the cold winter months.

Why then, is it not acceptable for truck drivers to be comfortable in their work and home environments?

Many work environments provide for comfortable working conditions and that right should be provided across the board.

While there are strives made in new technology to address providing for comfort in the commercial vehicles, these great new technologies are very expensive and can range in the thousands of dollars. In our present economy, this expense is not cost effective.

There needs to be responsible legislature in place to protect the environment but it needs to be fair and consistent across the board and at a price that everyone can afford.

Missing Arrow Driver found

January 9, 5:53 PM, Dallas Trucking Examiner, Rhianna Weir

There is never a happier moment when a family is reunited with a loved one. John Eischens family announced today that they have heard from the missing Arrow driver and that he is okay.

While there are no details as to what had transpired, this article is to let all those who have been actively helping to search for this driver and loved one.

A big thank you to all of the men and women in the trucking industry, and the volunteers from OOIDA and Support for Stranded Arrow Drivers for their help in the search. A special thanks to Sirius Radio's Freewheelin, The Trucking Bozo, Evan Lockridge, Jonesy, and the Nemo show for helping to get the word out, and to the Anna, TX and Montana Police Departments for their immediate action.

Conclusion:

This book is short and is meant to be. It is meant to introduce the world of trucking to the general public and those interested in the trucking industry. It is meant to be as informative as possible. Due to the nature of the book, it is impossible to provide a more in depth analysis of every aspect of trucking. To do so would hinder the true intent of the author; this is to provide insight into trucking.

While this book is short in length, it is not short in content. There is a lot of information to be absorbed. It is meant for the prospective student to gain general knowledge. It is also meant to give the general public insight into a world they only wondered about but were afraid to approach a truck driver and ask their question. This book is for them!

Being a truck driver has its advantages, rewards and benefits. Driving has it disadvantages but only if you let it become a problem. If you follow the rules of the road and do your best, your job is a great one. I hope the information in this book has been helpful and I see you out here soon.

Answers to Trivia Questions from Chapter Three

Answers:

1. Highway 80; California

2. Highway 40; 35 mph

3. North Carolina, Tennessee, Arkansas, Oklahoma, Texas, New Mexico, Arizona, California

4. Utah

5. 55 mph

6. Grants Pass

7. California

8. Nevada

9. Exit 60

10. Do you really have to look for the answer here?

11. You just got invited for a sleep over!

12. Utah

13. Road Dog

14. North Carolina; highway 40

15. 50 mph

16. 8

17. No

18. Texas

19. Only the reader can answer this question

www.ingramcontent.com/pod-product-compliance
Lightning Source LLC
Chambersburg PA
CBHW071230170526
45165CB00003B/1061